THE
SHADOWS UNDER
THE LAMP
essays on
September 11 and Afghanistan

RONALD CREAGH
and
SHARIF GEMIE

FREEDOM PRESS
LONDON

Published in 2003 by
Freedom Press
84B Whitechapel High Street
London E1 7QX

© 2003 Freedom Press

ISBN 1 904491 03 0

Cover design by Clifford Harper and Jayne Clementson
Typeset by Jayne Clementson

Printed in Great Britain by Aldgate Press
Units 5/6 Gunthorpe Workshops, Gunthorpe Street, London E1 7RQ

THE SHADOWS
UNDER THE LAMP

CONTENTS

Foreword   9

Ronald Creagh
The Spectacular and the Sacred
Notes for a debate on terrorism   11

Sharif Gemie
Afghanistan 2001-02
The land at the edge of the future   45

FOREWORD

T HIS BOOK STARTED IN THE HOURS after the 11th September attack. I was stunned by that event, and had no idea how to understand it. I was therefore amazed when, a few days later, Ronald Creagh circulated a response, written in French. I translated his analysis, and it was published in *Anarchist Studies* 10.1 (April 2002). In the last months of 2001 Ronald Creagh wrote a longer analysis of the event, which I reviewed for *Anarchist Studies*. In the course of 2002 I was moved by events in Afghanistan. These were very far from my academic specialism (by training, I'm a historian of nineteenth century France), but events seemed at once so important and so misunderstood that I felt that almost any response to publicise the tragedy that was unfolding there would be worthwhile. A number of Afghan friends were extremely supportive, and helped suggest sources of information and lines of enquiry.

This book was then put together in the last months of 2002 and the first months of 2003. The first half is my translation of Ronald Creagh's pamphlet, which has been checked by the author. A few sentences have been slightly changed, but it is substantially the text that he produced late in 2001. The second half is my essay on Afghanistan, written in

January and February 2003. Readers should not forget the dates when these texts were written: history is moving fast, and writing on these events can age far more quickly than authors intend.

Lastly, I'd like to dedicate this booklet to the memory of two absent colleagues. The first is Sayd Bahaouddin Majrooh, an Afghani academic who was assassinated in exile in February 1988, and from whose writing I drew the saying which forms the title of this work. While I'm sure he would have disapproved of much that this text contains, I want to signal how much I was inspired by the lucidity of his writing and his ability to succeed in that most difficult of tasks: self-criticism. Secondly, I'd like to dedicate this work to John Moore, who worked with me on *Anarchist Studies* and who died in 2002 of a heart attack. I'm certain that John would not have agreed with much (or most) of this work, but I'd guess that he would have enjoyed the paradoxical beauty of Majrooh's saying.

Sharif Gemie
July 2003

THE SPECTACULAR AND THE SACRED

NOTES FOR A DEBATE ON TERRORISM

A GENERATION OF AMERICANS will forever remember 11th September 2001 as one of the greatest acts of violence in their history. The surprise attack at New York killed thousands, many more than the number of deaths at Pearl Harbour. More importantly, it symbolised a clash between two visions of the world, one commercial, the other sacred.

The vulnerability of the American Republic was demonstrated by the massive loss of life and the collapse of one of its most emblematic monuments. This cataclysm forced the whole country to rethink its geo-political vision and its international connections.

Far from being limited to the territory and sphere of influence of the USA, this unexpected change in policy effected world history. Disconcerting emotions, as well as a political culture shaped by ideological preferences, encouraged Americans to demand 'surgical strikes'. Unfortunately, in this case, the doctor had arrived at a faulty diagnosis.

We need to reconstruct the evidence, develop analysis, and propose new points for debate. This preliminary study is divided into two sections: Part one, 'The Earthquake', examines the evidence, considers the causes of the attack, and surveys its consequences. The second part, 'The State within the State', turns to a different issue: the contemporary formation of the state and its attitude to terrorism. The complexity of the situation certainly requires multiple forms of analysis.

THE EARTHQUAKE

We will start with a critical analysis of the evidence, as filtered by the American media and public opinion. This will include a brief discussion of a rarely considered group, the Arab-Americans. We will examine two possible causes of the attack: American policies and Islamist protest. Lastly, the attack's consequences suggest that we must broaden our analysis to include a global perspective on US policies in south-west Asia, concentrating on their economic dimension.

THE FACTS

The Slaughter on 11th September 2001

This was one of the most spectacular events ever: almost unreal, it unfolded in front of the cameras' lenses, far worse than anything that a Hollywood horror film could contain. It was almost Pompeii: a night of fire and ashes descended on New York. A vast crowd had to leave their cars and cross the Manhattan bridges on foot in the stifling heat. Events in Washington were just as tragic, although they were downplayed by the media. For instance, one employee happened to be outside the west face of the Pentagon, where renovation work, costing $258m and lasting three years, had just been completed. He saw a plane suddenly swoop towards the building, right to the office where his wife worked.

The people involved showed an exemplary sense of solidarity and self-control. Hundreds of lives were saved by the *absence* of panic on the stairways of the twin towers. New York's citizens demonstrated something which no one had suspected of them: their deep generosity, their real sense of care for others. Later opinion polls showed that New Yorkers had no greater wish for revenge than the rest of the country.

Whatever one's politics, everyone must feel a sense of compassion for the victims' families and, above all, for those who were in those fateful planes, and for the planes' crews. One thinks of the agony suffered by the air stewards who work in such a confined environment.[1] Even those left-wing critics who are obsessed by the need to always prove America guilty cannot justify these crimes. Any political protest which showed no compassion for these victims would be manipulative and improper. It should never be forgotten that those who suffered most were ordinary people: caretakers, cooks, firefighters and paramedics.

The Media

The 11th September attacks were clearly a most important media event. Warner Brothers even rushed to buy exclusive rights to the images for some blockbuster which will probably make millions. The various press agencies issued more news flashes in a single day than they usually do in a whole year.

This unknown assailant had turned televisual imperialism back against American society. The attack ended the long series of triumphant portrayals of GIs and their campaigns across the four corners of the world, but above all in African and Arab countries. This was a sensational act that neither the Nazis nor the Japanese kamikazes had managed. For a moment, it shocked the whole world.

Despite their claims, the media did not respond with a rolling news coverage, but by a hysterical and repetitive bombardment of the same images. They constantly re-played pictures of the joy felt by some Palestinians, but they did not show the celebrations in Pakistan, and they avoided the Palestinian village in which there was an all-night wake for the dead. Much more was said about the civilian victims in New York than about the military personnel killed in the Pentagon. There was hardly a word about the millions of gold bars in the World Trade Centre's basement, beyond a discreet statement that there was no reason to be concerned for them. They were recovered later.[2]

The tele-evangelists interpreted this mini-apocalypse as an act of God. It was a punishment on America for having accepted women's liberation, birth control, homosexuality and other 'crimes'.

These attacks created a dramatic wave of emotion. This understandable reaction was reinforced by the American tendency to measure the gravity of an event by the number of corpses: as if one death wasn't already too many. An obsession with statistics intensified the passions caused by the attack. And immediately, each spectator reacted like a counter-terrorist, thinking of revenge rather than justice. Instead of considering the possibility of a non-violent framework for a response, extreme solutions against the alleged enemy were immediately discussed.[3]

Some commentators have criticised the media for only showing concern when American citizens are killed. Elsewhere, particularly when those who die come from a hostile country, the number of deaths is not mentioned or, it should be noted, they are presented merely as 'collateral damage'. Statistics cited by an enemy are dismissed as unverifiable estimates. For example, the Gulf War was presented as a conflict without deaths, as if dead Iraqis were not also human beings.

The whole of America was so traumatised that public libraries everywhere began to display books on grief management. Yet some observers, especially those living abroad, thought that this was a lost opportunity for the American population finally to open their eyes on their country's foreign policy and its damaging effects.

Belligerent action was promptly prescribed. The old veterans of military policy, Dick Chaney, Colin Powell, Donald Rumsfeld and even

Condoleezza Rice, the team who had worked with Bush senior, rapidly appeared on the television screens. Significantly, this line-up was mostly made up by personalities from the Department of Defence, rather than the Department of Justice. Such a staging was designed to create a national consensus: the crime must have been perpetrated by foreigners; America now had its martyrs. Furthermore, the use of the word 'terrorism' suggested at first sight an unequal relationship between a criminal and an innocent victim. Following Kissinger, who referred to Pearl Harbour, the President linked the two ideas of terrorism and war. Terrorism called for war and the retaliatory warfare could therefore also be terroristic, unbound by international war legislation. Nothing was said about the context: there was no serious analysis and no-one could designate any country as the possible aggressor. Even the political or religious identity of these new kamikazes was unknown.

Finally, when the name of Osama Bin Laden was pronounced, the US President immediately responded with the language of Far West mythology: Osama was wanted dead or alive. It was like going back in time, to the era of vigilantes. Bush did not mention any need for a court, international or otherwise. The victims would impose their own justice. All that was left was to wait for the next Saint Valentine's Day, so that the forces of the law could corner all their enemies and wipe them from the face of the earth.

In other words, Bush was leading the nation to war. All other options were rejected without explanation. In particular, there was no discussion of a police operation under international supervision.

The presumed leader of the attack, Osama Bin Laden, was in Afghanistan. The US administration demanded that the Taliban authorities should hand over all those in charge of Bin Laden's organisation, without any negotiation. This amounted to a threat, and there was no guarantee that compliance would absolve the Taliban from any future demands.

The Taliban asked to see the evidence before accepting these conditions. In international law, a request to hand over a suspect can only be enforced if there are bilateral extradition treaties between the two countries in question and, most importantly, if the relevant evidence has been presented to the legitimate authorities. Washington refused to do this. The Taliban decided not to hand over Bin Laden.

American Opinion

All the opinion polls show the solidarity that Americans felt with Bush. They also revealed that Americans were clearly in favour of a bombing campaign, even of a land-based campaign in Afghanistan, and that they expected new attacks. Furthermore, there was a majority in favour of a war with Iraq, although this stance may have been a passing expression of the anxiety which peaked during the threats of bacteriological attacks.

On 1st October 2001, 42% of the US population said that the attacks had made them feel depressed, 21% that they had difficulty in concentrating on their work and 18% were suffering from insomnia. 73% were worried about future attacks and 10% – about nineteen million people – had cancelled or were considering cancelling a flight.[4]

Pacifist feeling only emerged later. The anti-war demonstrations on 29th September attracted few people: a significant fifteen thousand in Washington, but only three hundred in New York. 75% did consider that the media should also broadcast the opinions of those who thought that the USA was partly to blame for the tragedy. The dominant feeling, however, expressed by 72%, was anger.

Those who had lived under the spell of the consumer society suddenly woke up to the realities of a bigger world. To go back to their dreams, they were called to return to the capitalist economy: investment and consumption became signs of patriotism.

The directors of Clear Channel, the world's biggest radio chain, decided to ban John Lennon's *Imagine*, Paul Simon's *Bridge over Troubled Water* and anything by Rage Against the Machine. The big television channels did not cover any of the anti-war demonstrations.

For the first time in American history, Washington asked the media to impose censorship: the government requested that Bin Laden's speeches should be banned, and the five biggest television news channels agreed. By not broadcasting the Muslim leader's speeches, the television channels left the population in complete ignorance about his intentions. This silence created an opportunity for the Al Jazeera channel from the Emirate of Qatar which became, in October 2001, the Arab equivalent of CNN.

The American media's patriotic proclamations gave, however, a false impression. One should not confuse the support offered to the victims, and even to soldiers, with nationalism and its inevitable accompanying xenophobia. There was a similar confusion concerning the attackers: Muslims were blamed for the actions of Islamists, Taliban for the actions of their leaders who, in turn, were to be treated in the same way as Bin Laden.

The television images of the bombing campaign in Afghanistan had the same flaws as those shown during the Gulf War. The photos of bombed military camps were hardly convincing: they showed sites which could easily be captured, places that had been abandoned long ago and – probably – a fair few deliberately deceptive shots. The television channels did not state when images had been shot, nor which footage had been circulated by the army for propagandistic reasons. Often the translation of Pashtun refugees' words bore little resemblance to their original speeches.

The manner in which the attacks on 11th September were reported divided Arab-Americans from the rest of the population. Many of them felt threatened: some were actually attacked.

The Arab-Americans

A few facts about this little-known group: the first significant Arab migration to the USA began in 1875 and continued until 1920. It was then limited by the new quota system. Migration revived after 1940, as a result of the conflicts in the Middle East.

There are about three million Arabs in the USA: slightly less than 1% of the total population. The great majority were born there, and they can be found in all the states, with particular concentrations in California, Michigan and New York. Sharing a common culture, they belong to different religious groups: Muslim, Christian, Druze and Jewish. The majority are Catholic or Orthodox Christians. The proportion of Arab-Americans who have been to University is higher than the American average. They are also active voters. In 1996, 54% of them voted for Bill Clinton, and 38% for his opponent, Bob Dole.

There are many more Muslims in the USA: about six million in total. They form distinct groups, particularly among Afro-Americans. They should not be confused with the Nation of Islam, who represent a quite different political and religious culture. Particularly during the prosperous decades of the 1980s and 1990s, the Saudi government has sponsored campaigns to convert American Muslims to the Wahhabi form of Islam which is dominant in Saudi Arabia. They have also tried to influence Afro-Americans offering, for example, free journeys to Saudi Arabia and training for imams. It seems, however, that despite the Saudis' contributions to mosques, they have had little effect and that their influence is in decline.

Whatever the effects of 11th September on particular segments of American population, the event was something radically new in world history. Some science-fiction works, and even some children, had imagined such an attack, but no one had thought of using civilian aircraft.

It seems that the Nazis may have been the first to consider attacks on the symbols of American power. Josef Goebbels, the Minister of

Propaganda, discussed plans for the destruction of the Empire State Building, alongside other targets. His plans involved missiles guided by kamikaze pilots. The Nazis' secret services even found some volunteers, including the celebrated Hannah Reitsch, and began planning an operation. The course of the war, however, forced the Third Reich to drop the project.

Such points may suggest that the 11th September attack should be considered as an act of war. But no state has been identified as the aggressor, and this anonymity makes it difficult to understand the meaning of this insane act.

THE CAUSES: BLOWBACK?

Since the end of the Cold War, American policies have become more unilateral and more indifferent to other nations. In this respect the USA is no different from past superpowers. America has often been criticised for its moralistic and patronising discourse, and its willingness to sacrifice diplomacy to economic interests, which have become the beginning and end of its policies.

Were these terrible attacks a response to American foreign policy? In any case, Washington has rediscovered strategic considerations and economic interests are again related to geo-political strategies.

The Politics of a Superpower

Although it is a hegemonic power, the USA is not the omnipotent power that it is often imagined to be, or that it allows others to think it is. It certainly cannot do all that it wants to do, even within its sphere of influence. This is because the world has changed: people are increasingly differentiating themselves from their governments. And even lackeys sometimes revolt against their masters.

The date of 11th September reminds us of another 11th September, during which aircraft attacked the symbols of political power, buildings collapsed and people ran from the inferno. This was in 1973, in Santiago, Chile. This terror was organised with the USA's assistance. Following the assassination of the democratically elected President Allende, this terror inaugurated the bloody dictatorship of General Pinochet, who is guilty of crimes for which he has never been tried.

In the last twenty years the USA has bombed Libya, Grenada, Panama, Somalia, Haiti, Afghanistan, Sudan, Iraq and Yugoslavia. Many of these attacks have been aimed at Muslim societies, and several of them break international law. They have made the USA hated, particularly when they have resulted in victims. On the other hand, the USA was aware of the 1994 genocide in Rwanda, and they did not participate in the UN attempts to maintain peace.

Many on the left, in the United States and abroad, have invited American public opinion to ponder the significance of the 11th September attacks in comparison with the previous aggressions carried out by the USA. The nation was cold-bloodedly responsible for millions of deaths throughout the world, it was argued, and this incursion in her territory was somehow a response and a reminder of the evils committed by the USA. The 11th September attacks could be considered as 'blowback', to use the CIA's term to describe the negative repercussions of an initiative. There were many throughout the world who felt that the 11th September was a fair response for the humiliations and oppressions imposed, supported or tolerated by a superpower which wants to be the world's policeman.

But where did this revenge come from?

Many looked to Palestine. Bush did not seem to care what happened to the Palestinians, and he allowed the most conservative Israelis to do as they wished. Was 11th September a response to this tragedy? The last speech by Bin Laden certainly referred to the Palestinians' plight, but it was used more as a mobilising argument than as a reason for actions. The attacks had needed two years planning: in other words, they were first considered when the Israel-Palestinian negotiations, encouraged by Clinton, seemed to be succeeding. It seems, therefore, that we need to look elsewhere for their causes.

Islamist Protest

We should also consider a third 11th September: that of 1683, when Muslims were defeated outside the walls of Vienna by the King of Poland and his allies. The Turkish invasion was decisively stopped. Muslim civilisation, which had contributed so much to the development of Christian Europe, had suffered both a military and a cultural defeat. 1683 was the beginning of a long eclipse, and it is possible that some anti-modernists recall this with bitterness, though this coincidence in the dates is probably irrelevant if one refers to the Moslem calendar.[5]

So, was this a war between two civilisations, as some have claimed? Islamists were certainly counting on similar arguments to rally the Muslim and Arab masses to their cause. Huntingdon's book, *The Clash of Civilisations*, which popularised such ideas, is based on several questionable assumptions:

- If one can identify at least seven or eight world civilisations, then why should one reduce the axis of conflict to two of them?
- Both 'Christian civilisation' and 'Islamic civilisation' are abstractions. There is as much different between a French Catholic and a German Lutheran as there is between a Lebanese and a Saudi Muslim. One can only speak of a Christian or Islamic identity if one personifies these complex entities by single individuals such as Louis XIV or Saladin.
- The Arab world is not united, and only contains about 12% of the

world's Muslims. As for Islam: it includes some sharply different currents, some of which are engaged in long conflicts, such as that between Iran and Iraq.

• The 'clash of civilisations' thesis ignores the fruitful exchanges which have taken place between diverse religions.

However, a willingness to sacrifice one's life in a kamikaze attack can only be explained by some faith in the hereafter and therefore by a religious vision.

Muslim Theology

There are many interpretations of Islam and even many different Islamic fundamentalisms, as is the case in all religions and all ideologies.

Avoiding simplistic generalisations, we can make the following distinctions: not all Muslims are Islamists, not all Islamists are Taliban, and not all Taliban are terrorists. Religion can provoke wars, as has happened frequently throughout history, but this is not necessarily the case here.

France has benefited from a particular form of religious development. The Catholic church created the Inquisition and organised the Crusades. The separation of the Church and the State, finally enacted in 1905, was the result of the bloody battles dating back to the religious conflicts of the sixteenth and seventeenth centuries. Following the separation, the majority of Catholics then accepted some secular principles, and their leaders are a million miles from seeking to create a theocracy.

Islamic texts do not contain equivalent concepts concerning the relative positions of the Church and State. Muslims' concept of pluralism is quite different. They have never been willing to accord a full equality to believers from other religions, neither in theory nor in practice. But they do allow a degree of toleration to those who possess a partial truth, and such forms of toleration were rarely imitated by earlier forms of Christianity.

There were times when Muslims admired and respected Western civilisation. They saw its military superiority and then its advances in other areas. Muslims attempted to implement their own forms of modernisation and liberalisation, as happened in Turkey. Something similar can even be seen in the present-day Iranian Republic, with its written constitution, its elected assembly and even its ecclesiastical hierarchy: three institutions for which there is no precedent in Muslim history and no instructions in Islamic teaching.

This admiration for the West has faded, and today western culture is met with hostility and rejection. The propaganda issued by the two great mid-twentieth-century dictatorships, Nazi Germany and Soviet Russia, finally served to discredit all western initiatives. During the two world wars, Muslims could watch a civilisation tearing itself apart: a process which led to collective suicides and unprecedented devastation.

The western-inspired modernisation of Muslim countries certainly produced great wealth, but migrants from the west and tiny indigenous minorities profited most from these processes. Even in the case where these minorities expanded, they remained distinct from the mass of the population, marked off by different clothes and different lifestyles. The better-off elements were eventually assimilated into the ranks of the foreigners: they acted first as their agents, and then as their collaborators. Any political innovations introduced into such countries were equally discredited, as they were often merely inadapted imitations of foreign models.

Islamic Fundamentalism

Contemporary Islamic fundamentalism began with the Muslim Brothers, who started in Egypt in 1928. Hounded by Nasser, they found a refuge in Saudi Arabia, where their ideas were seen as compatible with the Saudis' Wahhabism and their extremely strict interpretation of Islam. They became more and more influential in Saudi schools and, exploiting their influence and the wealth of their new homeland, the Muslim Brothers then expanded into other countries.

The issues which most concern doctrinaire Islamists are not western wealth, social injustice or third world poverty: on this point, left-wing analysts are often mistaken. They do condemn corruption and insist in the duty of all Muslims to give one-tenth of their income to charity, but charity is not social justice, a belief in equal rights for all individuals, irrespective of age, sex, religion or inheritance, nor is it a rejection of forms of economic and corporate domination. These believers were first and foremost theocrats: they refused all separation of State and Church. If the faithful were Allah's servants, then the unbelievers must be his enemies. No Islamist dogmatist would ever accept that one of God's servants should be commanded by one of the enemy.

The fundamentalists fought two enemies: secularism and modernity.

a) The war against secularism was conscious and deliberate. A flood of Islamist writing denounced it as an evil, neo-pagan force, and blamed it on the Jews, the West or the USA. Bin Laden's biographers record that his rebellion began during the Gulf War, when he saw American troops based in Saudi Arabia, on the land that the Prophet had declared must never have two religions.

b) The struggle against modernity was certainly not a rejection of technical progress, but it fought the culture which accompanied it. In most cases, this was not a conscious, deliberate struggle. It opposed the deep transformations of the political, social, economic and even cultural structures of Islamic societies in the twentieth century, which had provoked a deep anger and an ill-defined resentment among the masses. Islamic fundamentalism gave these concerns a voice. Islam's religious culture inspired a sense of dignity, even among the most humble. It encouraged courtesy to strangers and a warm sense of community: attitudes which the westerners never seemed to adopt.

Social crises, disintegration and explosions of rage dragged these ancient and refined civilisations into searching through the works of the Prophet for texts which justified assassination and kidnapping.

It must be stressed that fundamentalism is certainly not the only Muslim tradition. There are many others, usually noticeably more tolerant, and we must hope that these will become dominant. Direct initiatives in this realm by Western states are usually counter-productive: Muslims must decide for themselves.

Islamist protest, which aimed to unite the whole of the Muslim world in a jihad against the rest of the world, chose to attack the vanguard of westernisation: the USA. The attack on the USA in turn provoked the American campaign in Afghanistan. Putting aside Bin Laden, the reasons for this attack were principally political and economic.

THE SEQUEL: THE ORIGINS OF THE THIRD WORLD WAR

Given the number of countries which were involved in the war against 'terrorism', it is no exaggeration to speak of a global conflict. The conflagration began long before Bin Laden's attacks. However, while Bin Laden's predecessors had mostly targeted Muslim governments that they considered had strayed too far from the path, Bin Laden chose to attack the principal enemies and so to unite in the same struggle all protest movements within Muslim nations. This approach clearly distinguished this conflict from other types of war.

It has already engendered important tactical changes in the United States policies and those of other major nations. The cold war was also a world confrontation, but without any bloody conflict between the belligerent powers. We can see these developments as marking the beginning of the Third World War. Islamic fundamentalism does not only target the USA, but all the countries who oppose it. Washington, reviving the schemas of the Cold War, has decided to take on whoever they decide to be a terrorist, anywhere in the world and irrespective of their sphere of influence. This conflict, however, is profoundly different from previous conflagrations, for it is based on asymmetric oppositions, secret systems of repression and it will probably include periods of respite.

The New American Agenda

When he got to power, Bush had an agenda: he would not get involved in nation-building abroad. He had used this point as a way of criticising Clinton, who had committed American troops in Somalia and then in the Balkans. Bush wanted to move away from the UN, to abandon the ABM treaty with the USSR in order to develop a new anti-missile system (the famous 'son of Star Wars'), to support Taiwan, and to leave Israel and Sharon free to negotiate as they wished with the Palestinians.

The President's policies quickly isolated the USA from some of the main international actors. The sanctions imposed on Iraq were criticised with increasing volume by Germany, France, Russia and China. Points of disagreement multiplied: Star Wars, the greenhouse effect and the international court. On several occasions, the USA was humiliated, often in the UN. The anti-globalisation movements acquired more support, demonstrating the gap between the populations and their governments.

Then, following the attacks of 11th September, there was a radical re-drafting of American foreign policy. This was an important turning point. The apostles of economic liberalisation fell silent, and there were demands for state intervention. Kissinger had made the defence of human rights a key tactic in the Cold War with the USSR: this policy was ended.[6] The earlier campaigns against dictatorships and corrupt governments were ended. Henceforth, all US foreign policy centred on a single issue: terrorism, as defined by Washington so that it included Cuba but left out Pakistan. The administration promptly decided to lift several economic embargoes and to supply weapons and military assistance to those countries that co-operated with its new policies, even when these countries were dictatorships. The White House no longer seemed concerned about the trials of Russian officers who had carried out atrocities in Chechnia. The Chamber of Representatives was prevented from passing a decree which would have put pressure on Sudan, a country which has been oppressing non-Muslims in its southern region for a decade.[7]

The US secret services suffered a deep crisis of confidence. How had dozens of agents been able to operate on American soil without the CIA, the FBI or any other service giving the slightest sign of alarm? No explanation was given for these failings, despite the fact that these services spent some $20bn each year. Instead, the various surveillance agencies saw their budgets massively increased: a measure which threatened civil liberties.[8]

Abroad, the situation seemed equally serious. Although intelligence services had been active in Afghanistan since 1998, they did not employ a single Pushtu speaker. No university in the USA offered courses in Pushtu, although it was possible to study Hittite, a language which has not been spoken for four thousand years.

Bush learnt new forms of speech. Having proclaimed a crusade, and then addressed America's problems in the language of the Wild West, announcing a punitive expedition like a vigilante, he was then forced to moderate his words. His stance underwent a painful revision.

As has often been the case in the USA, the opposition between hawks and doves re-surfaced. The hawks were to be found in the Pentagon. Among them were Richard Perle and Paul Wolfowitz, the Assistant

Secretary for Defence, who missed the good old days of the Cold War, and wanted "to put an end to terrorist states".[9] The doves were represented by Colin Powell, the secretary of State, who was supported by Donald Rumsfeld and Condoleezza Rice, National Security Advisor. Rice was to play a vital role: initially she did not appear to belong to either camp, and therefore winning her support for a particular policy could guarantee its adoption by the administration. The Pentagon was considering a large-scale campaign which might include the Hezbollah camps in Lebanon, and attacks on Iraq, although there was no proof that either had participated in the attacks of 11th September. On the other hand, Powell proposed sending special forces from the UK and USA, perhaps with assistance from Germany, from the French Foreign Legion and even from the Russians, to seize Bin Laden. He wanted more time to build up a wider coalition.

Both sides accepted that air strikes should be organised: a daft idea, when one considers how much agitation the 11th September attacks had caused in so many countries: Germany, Belgium, Holland, France, Britain, Greece, Syria, Chechnia, Russia, Iran, Egypt, the Arab Emirates, Lebanon, Saudi Arabia, Yemen, Malaysia, the Philippines and even the USA itself. Political, diplomatic, ideological and economic pressure – particularly on Bin Laden's sources of income – might have been more efficient in the long run. At worst, the American reprisals could lead to the deaths of thousands of civilians, without any chance of a military success because, according to the experts, Bin Laden would definitely have left his training camps. But the Americans were not seeking to punish their designated enemy. They had another aim: they wanted to install a government in Afghanistan which would be favourable to their international policies.

The air strikes in Afghanistan were designed to respond to the needs of the American collective unconsciousness, by staging a dramatisation of its power of coercion. The American willingness to act with only UK support also responded to a propagandistic imperative: the need to affirm the *pax americana* today, so as to guarantee economic benefits tomorrow.

In brief, the Bush administration had returned to the ideas of the Cold War. It aimed to identify an enemy and to assert a national mission; it divided the world into two camps: terrorists and friends; it wanted to solve political, social and economic problems by the gun; it cosied up to torturers and supplied arms to future aggressors on condition that they were allies today.

Afghanistan and the Great Game

American military aims remained confused. They were not dealing with a dictator or a nation, but with poorly defined international networks. Washington was going to intervene in a zone, Afghanistan, which many other countries – such as China, Russia, India and particularly Pakistan – thought was central to their interests. The Americans had to maintain a coalition and to keep quiet about their long-term aims so as not to disrupt the fragile consensus of concerned powers, and not to worry the Arab and Muslim countries.

In 2001, Afghanistan was divided between hostile factions. The Americans did not want to be forced into taking the responsibility for creating a new government: they were to be disappointed. Bush had frequently rebuked Clinton for failing to understand that it was not enough to win a war: you had to make sure that fighting would not begin again after your exit. Like his predecessors, Bush was going to have to learn the same lesson. The USSR's retreat from Afghanistan in 1989 had left behind a political vacuum which led to chaos. The Taliban and Bin Laden had exploited this situation. The US government was eventually forced to appeal to the UN: Bush made a confused reference to it in his first press conference after 11th September, on 11th October 2001.

This was a turning-point in US/Russian relations. Russia was growing less hostile to NATO. In principle, there was agreement: Russia offered access to its oil-fields as an alternative to those of the agitated Middle East. On 12th September 2001, the Russia secret services had even named the criminal: according to them, Bin Laden was the co-ordinator, and the attack had been planned by Jamiat-e Islamiya, based in Pakistan and Saudi Arabia,[10] who controlled over four hundred suicide pilots, and who were planning new attacks on American nuclear and space installations. Russia even went so far as to abandon its monitoring posts in Cuba and its naval base in Vietnam. Not only was the Cold War over, but the post-Cold War transition had also been completed.

Putin's support, however, meant difficult negotiations for Bush on the Anti-Ballistic Missile treaty. The Russian military were also worried by the presence of American and British soldiers in their former republic, Uzbekistan. This state, notable for its failure to respect human rights, refused to allow combat troops or bombers to leave from its territory into Afghanistan. This move, however, was probably no more than a bargaining ploy, aiming to secure greater American financial aid. Finally, American troops were stationed at Manas base in Kyrgyzstan and at the Karshi-Khanabad base in Uzbekistan during the Afghan campaign.

Russia and China had consolidated their grip on most of the ex-Soviet republics in Central Asia, and China had just granted $1m to Tadjikistan's army. Both countries were concerned by the entry of US forces into the region. Russia placed seven thousand soldiers on alert in Tadjikistan.

China wanted to be seen to be supporting the US campaign, but it also wanted concessions from Washington. This Chinese complained publicly about the US's multilateral policies, its initiatives which ignored the UN and its plan to create an anti-missile system. The Chinese, who 'only' have about twenty nuclear missiles capable of hitting the USA, far fewer than either America or Russia, may well have gained some concessions from the USA on these points. For instance,

Washington has made it clear that it does not support a unilateral declaration of independence by Taiwan.

The Russians and Chinese were certainly prepared to co-operate in the anti-terrorist campaign, but they rejected the selectivity of the US plans. According to them, the anti-terrorist campaign had to be global, and therefore should also target the separatists and terrorists of Chechnia (some of whom were Muslims trained in Afghanistan), of Tibet, of Taiwan and – immediately – the Muslim Uighr separatists who live in China, in the region directly to the east of Afghanistan. The Chinese also considered that the US campaign provided an unexpected boost to their lengthy struggle against the Xinjiang independence movement. Indeed, the word 'terrorist' was so vague that many governments could use it against their opponents: this happened in, for example, India, Egypt, Turkey, the Central Asian Republics and Iraq. The term could also be applied to the various armed struggles in Europe: in the Balkans, but also in Ireland, the Basque Country and Corsica. The term is a treacherous one. For example, it allowed the anti-democratic forces in Italy to stifle the anti-globalisation movement. Its use may well curtail civil liberties.

The change in American foreign policies caused the Bush administration many problems. Bush had pledged to co-operate with Pakistan, but this implied a re-consideration of American relations with India. He had given Sharon a free hand, but now he had to court the Arab states, and so he proclaimed his support for the eventual creation of a Palestinian state, and he put pressure on Sharon to renew negotiations with Arafat. Sharon's complaints that this was a new Munich, in which Israel was being sacrificed, clearly annoyed Bush.

While the television screens flew the flag, the situation was far more menacing than they suggested. No Muslim country participated in the attack on Afghanistan while, ten years earlier, there had been Arab countries supporting the war for Kuwait. Even in Kuwait, matters were far from simple. Semi-terrorist organisations were based there. The Kuwait government would only allow American forces to use its bases for attacks on Al-Qaeda or Afghan military positions. Elsewhere, Arafat looked for US support, while he was increasingly threatened by Hamas and Hezbollah. Iran was delighted: it could dismiss both the terrorists and the US government in the same breath, while watching American planes bomb the Taliban, one of Iran's greatest enemies. In Pakistan, the government was split. In Kashmir, according to Indian intelligence services, pan-Arabist groups such as Lashkar-i Taiyibah, armed by the Chinese, were ready to attack. In Saudi Arabia, America's most important ally, the corrupt and anti-democratic monarchy was wavering, and it finally decided not to co-operate in the American campaign: neither through intelligence co-operation nor through the repression of money-laundering. Lastly, the American campaign probably halted China's immediate economic development, although it could prove quite useful to the Chinese in the long-term. This at least was the opinion of international observers such as Chinese Colonels Qiao Liang' and Wang Xiangsui: two intellectuals whose book, *Unrestricted Warfare*, had suggested in 1999 that Bin Laden could attack the World Trade Centre.[11]

One would be wrong to conclude that the USA accepted all these risks out of a simple desire to avenge its dead at any cost. It had economic objectives in mind.

The Economic Dimension

President Bush was elected under conditions of debatable propriety. His victory had worried millions of Americans and a large proportion of world opinion. He was unable to find a solution to the growing problems of unemployment and financial decline. His administration had been criticised for its management of social security funds, and it was showing signs of internal division. On 20th August 2001, the *New York Times* expressed the ruling class's fears: the economy was sliding into recession across the world, in the USA, Europe, Japan and in some of the principal developing countries. The situation looked as bad as it had in 1973, at the start of the oil crisis. An executive from Ford declared that he did not expect any recovery for another twelve or eighteen months. The *New York Times* was therefore amazed by Bush's professed economic optimism. In fact, in August 2001 alone, the level of unemployment jumped from 4.5% to 4.9%: one million jobs were lost.

Two days before the fateful day on 11th September, a financial expert announced that confidence in the government was at an all-time low, that a 'reign of terror' was imminent, and that a major financial crisis was about to unfold. In fact, all these fears proved imaginary. There was an important bout of stock exchange speculation, led by experts, but nothing more.

Analysis of the attack's economic implications reveals many significant points. There are immense oil resources in Central Asia, and the USA is worried that Russia or Iran may be able to control their transport or distribution.

Russia has been seeking maritime access to its south for centuries. While Afghanistan is a landlocked country, Russia has considered projects for a pipeline to run through it. This was one reason for the Russian invasion of 1979. The Americans opposed them, because they were concerned about the extension of Soviet power in Asia. Today the independent republics of Turkmenistan, Uzbekistan and Kazakhstan are all very rich in oil, which would have to be distributed to the West along one of three routes: via the Caspian sea, via Russia or via the Caucasus.

Oil pipelines are already in operation, but all face a variety of threats of which the most important is war. These are unstable regions. Western interests therefore seek access via the Persian Gulf, as oil production is currently centred in the Middle East. A pipeline could pass through either Iran, or through Afghanistan and Pakistan. Given that Iran was hostile to the USA, Afghanistan seemed the best option.

Another possibility was a route through Turkey. But this would require access via Armenia (in conflict with Georgia), and the Caucasas and Azerbaijan, which are not stable areas.

Like all rich Texans, Bush is an oil man. His company had lost a lot of money but, following a series of deals, he was able to sell it for $2m in 1986 to another petrol company, Harkens Energy, which made money by buying up small companies close to bankruptcy. Bush became a consultant for Harkens. In 1990 Harkens Energy bought an off-shore oil rig in Bahrain: previously the company had only owned land-based installations. Bush then sold two-thirds of his shares, four days before Harkens announced major losses.[12] The US Vice-President, Dick Cheney, is also a director-general of Halliburton, the biggest oil-field services company in the world. This company sold equipment to Iraq, despite the UN sanctions. The oil industries made the biggest contributions to Bush's election campaign, and the majority of his ministers have connections with either the oil or transport industries.

These points suggest the extent to which the administration had economic interests in Afghanistan. Was Bin Laden's attack simply an opportunity which they seized? Their interests certainly help explain the US's preference for a war rather than recourse to an international tribunal and an appeal to the UN.

STATES WITHIN STATES

TERRORISM

'Terrorism' is first and foremost the use of brute force to serve a political end. It is not the only form of political violence: the shameless exploitation of unorganised workers, or the economic strangulation of a nation are both equally reprehensible forms of violence, even if one cannot, strictly speaking, categorise either of them as terrorism.

The 11th September attack was a conservative, authoritarian, right-wing form of terrorism because, rather than aiming at a symbolic target and attempting to avoid deaths, it killed without discrimination, like the infamous attack on Bologna Station. Such attacks are elements which contribute to a psychological war, attempting to stifle crowds through blind terror. There have been many examples of such terrorism, such as the attacks on tourists in Egypt.

Anti-globalisation activists face similar problems, for the frequent, heavy-handed and arbitrary attacks on their movement have the same aim of terrorising a political force.

The causes of terrorism are multiple and complex, varying according to time and place. But, to simplify, one can link today's terrorism, directly or indirectly, to globalisation.

THE GLOBALISATION OF IMPUNITY

Globalisation, as directed by the World Bank, has brought about debt, unemployment and the decline of traditional economic sectors. It has fractured social relations and, finally, it has created intolerable situations in many countries. The impoverishment of their governments and the pressures on their societies to become more competitive have reduced spending on health, education and social services. The shrinking of these resources has slowed development and led to the spreading of epidemics and diseases, and ultimately widened the gap between rich and poor nations.

Some sociologists justify this process on the grounds that these societies have passed from the coercive social relations of the village to the relative freedom provided by purely commercial relations. But while these observations may have some relevance to the experience of the richer countries, they do not apply to the poor, for in these countries there is hardly any commerce. Instead, this intolerable situation is marked by the dislocation of all social relations. An explosion of migrations in all directions is the inevitable result, involving the illegal smuggling of people and the re-structuring of social solidarities. States are no longer in control: sometimes they are not even significant agents. The economies are shaped by religious and secular networks, formed by multi-nationals, drug cartels, mafias and armed groups, capable of investing and withdrawing their capital at lightning speed.

Networks are spreading across the world: sometimes they take the form of constellations, affinity groups, virtual communities, alliance or coalitions. Such structures are most common in the richer countries, and here they are often quite egalitarian. In the poorest countries, on the other hand, hierarchic social formations evolve: neo-feudalisms, potentates, mafias, tribal organisations ... To this list we could add more primitive groupings, almost mobs, such as suburban gangs or Afghan warlords' armies. These associations, often oriented towards a mythic past, are the means by which the poor can form by themselves what we might term mediating institutions.

Globalisation, by making divisions more severe and by fracturing social relations, has aroused in the humiliated masses a vague resentment. It has only left the poor with the last scraps: religion and ethnicity, the cultural myths to which they are loyal. These myths in turn stimulate new conflicts from which many terrorisms develop. Alternative financial networks, like the charities organised and financed by Saudi Arabia, then substitute parallel structures for official governments. These are grafted onto new social formations. These resulting new right-wing terrorisms are often not totalitarian. Walter Laqueur classifies them as sub-statist or pseudo-statist.[13] They develop from social formations that are independent from any existing State. We therefore prefer to use another term to describe them: they are proto-States.

PROTO-STATES

Several social formations have created a particular type of para-legal status. Groups such as the IRA, FIS, ETA, etc., while quite different in nature, share the same logic that we will term 'proto-statist', a prefix borrowed from the Greek 'prôtos', first. They are, in fact, states in the process of formation, as can be seen by their objectives, their thinking and their structures. They want to constitute themselves as nations, and they adopt the most basic forms of the State, such as the management of people and resources, and the use of violence to achieve their ends. Normally they include two distinct wings, often independent of each other, which claim to be completely separate: a military wing, more concerned with fighting that with political concepts, and a political wing. Political theorists who have eyes for no one but existing, recognised states as their models, often ignore their proto-statist nature.

In the present case, the Al-Qaeda groups, directed by Bin Laden and others, were originally sustained by a number of states. This organisation was financed by the USA and some Arab countries who were happy to divert their own oppositions by letting them leave for Afghanistan where – the rulers hoped – they would be crushed by Russian tanks. These calculations were mistaken. Instead, these Arabo-Afghan hordes contributed to the resurrections of a new medievalism, marked by the return of the *condottieri*, the mercenary chiefs. This privatisation of war is one small aspect of the more general process of privatisation. Already, in the banana republics of South America or in the Gulf, wars serve the interests of multinationals and petrol companies. In Africa, they are increasingly fought by private armies, organised by millionaires, multinationals, governments of rich countries and secret services. Today, these social formations operate with their own mercenaries, as can be seen in Africa and elsewhere.

Multinationals, secret armies and the governments of the rich countries exploit the weakness of the State's structures and the social structures of the Third World, to finance organisations that, sooner or later, will resemble proto-states. This was the case with the Islamist military formations of Al-Qaeda which – it is said – were inspired by or financed by Bin Laden.

The Taliban were financed by the USA until, in 1984-85, it became clear from leaks from Soviet intelligence services, that the USSR was unable to sustain a war in Afghanistan. Washington supplied Stinger missiles to the mujahdin, who were then able to bring down Soviet helicopters. The Soviet generals slowly realised that the war was over. But, meanwhile, the mujahdin had grown into an Arab Foreign Legion. When, at the end of the war, the CIA offered to buy back their weapons, it met a curt refusal.

We are not witnessing what Clausewitz called the 'decomposition of substantial war', when some form of delirium is replacing political aims. The Al-Qaeda groups are not guerrillas. They do not fight to liberate territory. Instead, they have a distinctive political goal: the resurgence of a past which has been revived a hundred times over but never realised. They aim to constitute Great Islam, rich in unquestionable dogmas, indisputable theocracies, a billion believers and, in the future, most of the world's oil reserves. Their fantasies resemble those held by all nationalists, but they differ in their content. Their violence is like state violence: it is right-wing, it aims to spread panic, to kill without discrimination. In many ways, they resemble the mafia: with the important qualification that the mafia has no intention of bringing down the government.

Commentators speak knowledgeably about 'terrorist bases' but, in reality, their centres are quite different from orthodox military practices: all they need is some land on which they can indoctrinate people. No need for wealth: terrorist equipment can be knocked together with the most basic material – a few nails, the simplest nuclear technology, home-made biological weapons ...

Historically, the first biological combats were the poisoning of the enemy's wells. When the USA was still a British colony, the colonists gave the Indians blankets impregnated with smallpox. In 1984, the disciples of Bhagwan Shree Rajneesh spread salmonella in the restaurants of Oregon state: 751 people were poisoned. A decade later, the Japanese cult Aun Shinrikyo spread sarin, a toxic gas, in the Tokyo underground. Economic and military weapons, including weapons of mass destruction, are now available to everyone.

This new world order is particularly frightening for the USA, the country which has done most to destroy all the borders, to create a world market, to promote the freedom of circulation of communications, peoples and commodities. The American superpower possesses a colossal destructive power, but it is partly unusable – for example, its nuclear weapons – and partly ineffective in the case of a conflict with a small state: a particularly frustrating situation.

Globalisation has fragmented communities; the inner cities have become zones of concern; the mass media have created a rootless cosmopolitanism, destroying local groups in order to profit invisible, virtual communities, linked only by a common culture: see, for example, the charismatic attraction of a Hitler, a Kennedy, Princess Di or Bin Laden.

The absence of a true public sphere, in which local communities could take decisions, has been made worse by the one-way mass media, in which the expression of ideas and projects is reserved for elites. All at once, the frontier between the public and the private has been blurred. Questions as complex and delicate as abortion or the consumption of a particular substance are resolved through set-piece battles between opposed organisations. The result can be seen in the USA, where the threats to doctors who performs abortions have become so common that they are no longer counted.

CONCLUSION

The shift from a clearly defined field of conflict to a zone of more or less secret networks and transnational police is far too easily accepted by people when they hear the words 'police', 'society', and 'terrorism'. Instead of accepting this shift, we need to reconsider the nature of geopolitical cultures. While democracies sleep, their rulers act in a despicable manner abroad, or allow despicable acts to be carried out with impunity, encouraging smuggling, speculation and a daily terrorism in the name of the State.

Within countries, the repression of a pseudo-terrorism serves to limit further civil liberties. The threat of a party or a leader not being re-elected is hardly sufficient to make good the damage committed by the secret services or other agents in the ex-colonies. After all, Bin Laden is not the only Frankenstein conceived by the CIA. Democratic inspection of all the work of the secret services and the intelligence agencies is urgently needed. This will only happen if a popular mobilisation goes beyond particular group interests, and even beyond national interests, and begins to consider foreign policy, even in peace time – above all, when one hears the phrase 'non-conventional war'. This is still a war, just as violence, targeted, surgical or otherwise, remains violence.

A great deal of blood has been shed and will continue to be shed for pipelines in Central Asia and the Causasas. But it should never be forgotten that Afghanistan does not belong to the Americans, the Russians, the Chinese, the Pakistanis or the Iranians, nor even to the Taliban. Afghanistan belongs to all the men, women and children who live there.

The international appetite for this region's riches, and the battles between states to gain access to them, demonstrate all too clearly the evils of a world run by statist structures, by transnational companies and by the market system. For example, the USA's structural weaknesses are a result of a population living beyond its means. American families and businesses are in debt, the country is to blame for much of the world's pollution, and the American lifestyle, offered to so many as a model, can only result in disaster. If the Chinese attain the same levels of consumption, the planet will explode. For these reasons, social ecology has an important role to play in the prevention of terrorism.

The general uprooting of the work force, to be placed as the world's merchants require, can only favour the capillary propagation of all the extremisms. Yet international migration could be an opportunity for the planet if, where it starts, it is the result of a free choice and, where it ends, it is greeted by an acceptance of difference which is something more than indifference. Migrants and hosts could offer each other reciprocal training in toleration. Future generations could re-think their roots and their mixings. A collective sense of blood-links tends to lead to intransigent politics: we need to create new collective myths.

The dismantling of proto-States and their imperial accomplices pose serious questions for all who work for peace. How can this challenge be met? How can emancipatory movements be helped without creating new states and encouraging new feudalisms? Social struggles must develop 'soft' concepts of social and territorial space, allowing the participation of all concerned, in subtle, temporary institutions, networks rather than hierarchies, with a full sense of exchanges between participants, and still allowing, in the last instance, each individual and each minority the right to decide when an ethical issue is raised.

The present crisis shows that the disciples of economic liberalisation will always be willing to demand the State's help: this institution is as necessary to the free market as water is to a fish. The Stock Exchange was saved from a crash by the American Federal Reserve, the European Central Bank and the central banks of the world's principal countries. Hundreds of billions of dollars were injected.

And yet ... States are no longer what they were, and their actions can only lead to a dead end. For example, the creation of a Jewish State has not resolved any problems, and there were Jews predicting this before 1914.

We are not completely powerless. We can act against terrorism and war, but only on condition that we do not rely on the State's broken force or on multinationals. The crime of 11th September cannot be judged by a State, by the UN (which is just a collection of States), or by some 'popular' tribunal on the model of the Jacobin or Bolshevik terrors. It is up to us to propose the creation of a truly international justice, into which the best values of our societies can flow.

The future depends on the growth of independent, non-governmental organisations: on their coalitions or, still better, their free federation. The fall of the Berlin wall has shown the existence of a range of new international agents, aside from the superpowers and multi-nationals. The State is dying, and is being replaced by neo-feudalist warfare. But non-governmental organisations and transnational social movements are also developing, successfully acting as killjoys and creating a new agitational ethic.

These young, rising movements will soon be plagued by representatives of political parties, thirsty for votes or hungry to swallow them up. Little oligarchs and junior despots will grow among them. We can only meet these challenges by beginning a new epoch of free federations, based on an anti-hierarchic ethic and the spread of cheerfully egalitarian networks.

Lastly, when the old institutions lose their credibility, it is time to look for alternatives. Let's start modestly, by restoring the social fabric around us, and welcoming our own marginals. Multiply collective autonomies; federate. Everything needs to be created: isn't that a thought?

1. The press has hardly mentioned the tens of thousands of airline employees who were dismissed after 11th September, often with no compensation. On the other hand, the shareholders of these companies have pocketed thousands of dollars, generously provided by the American state with the avowed aim of refloating the companies. On the number of redundancies, see hrlive.com/layoff/.

2. *Figaro*, 14th September 2001.

3. Paul R. Pillar, *Terrorism and US Foreign Policy* (Washington: Brookings Institution Press, 2001), chapter 1.

4. For these polls, see polling report.com/terror.htm

5. Christopher Hitchens, 'Blaming Ben Laden First', *Minority Report*, 22nd October 2001.

6. Brzenzinski also claimed that he was the author of this idea. See his interview with Isabelle Girard, *L'Evènement du jeudi*, 8th January 1998, pages 50-51.

7. The Sudan Peace Act, supported by a right-wing Christian coalition, by trade unions and by the Congressional Black Caucus, aimed to stop the war of the Arab National Islamic Front against the Sudanese People's Liberation Army, which was fighting for self-determination. See Jim Lobe and Abid Aslam, 'The Terrible Trade-Offs', 25th September 2001, web@fpif.org

8. Hardly any funds were dedicated to anti-terrorist measures in 1995. By 1997 $130m were allocated, $1.5bn in 2000, and $11bn were proposed in 2001, *before* the events of 11th September!

9. Deputy Secretary of Defence Paul Wolfowitz, at a 13th September [2001] briefing, in stark contrast to Powell's statement, called for "ending states who sponsor terrorism". *The Washington Dispatch* http://www.washingtondispatch.com/article_56.shtml. Cf. 'The war on terrorism is a global war, and one that must be pursued everywhere'. World Affairs Council, San Francisco, California, 6th December 2002

10. The American Foreign Policy Council, *Russia Reform Monitor*, Special Issue 13th September 2001.

11. *China Reform Monitor* No. 408, 25th September 2001

12. Among the many other business relations of the Bush family, one ought to remember the Carlyle Group, for whom George Bush Sr. and John Major were in Saudi Arabia a few months before 11th September.

13. Walter Laqueur, 'Postmodern Terrorism: New Rules For An Old Game', *Foreign Affairs*, September/October 1996.

AFGHANISTAN 2001-02

THE LAND AT THE EDGE OF THE FUTURE

I N FRONT OF ME IS A PICTURE of a blue-veiled woman standing among what appears to be a large pile of rubble. Looking more closely, one can see that these stones are actually ruins of buildings: doors, walls, and places for windows can be detected. Such poignant images from Afghanistan have been published frequently in the press over the past months. They easily a evoke a sense of the desolation and of the strangeness of this lost country, whose peoples, customs and experiences seem so different from the norms of the twenty-first century West. Almost without thinking, we label Afghanistan as 'medieval', 'barbaric', even 'stone age', and we consider its people as if they were cursed by history to be the permanent, silent victims of greater processes.

This essay aims to reverse such perspectives: Afghanistan is not located in our past, but in our future; its peoples are not eternally the passive recipients of tyranny: they have tried to create new freedoms. The events which have taken place there over the past months are not examples of a strange history of a strange people, but telling indications of the manner in which *our* world is evolving.

'There is always darkness under the lamp', say the Afghans. Their country has been 'under the lamp' for twenty-five years: it has revealed much darkness.

LIBERATED AFGHANISTAN?

At the end of 2001, a soldier from the victorious Northern Alliance was interviewed about his hopes for the coming year. Twenty-six years old, he had been a full-time soldier since he was seventeen. He sounded optimistic, and his new year hopes were almost banal: he looked forward to "peace, a wife, children, money – this year could be the best year of my life".[1] He wanted to find work in an office, where he could put down his Kalashnikov and pick up a pen.

Many Afghans had similar hopes at the beginning of 2002. The Taliban, who had implemented the most repressive policies that it is possible to draw from Islam, had been easily defeated. Women were able to take off their *burqas*, men could shave their beards.[2] Newspapers and radio stations emerged, slowly but surely, often with help from international donors. Videos of the Bollywood films beloved by Afghans were back on sale in street stalls and roadside shops. In January 2002 a concert was given in Kabul, the Afghan capital, for the first time in six years. It took place in the ruins of the Nindari theatre: more than a thousand men, women and children watched anti-Taliban sketches and joined in songs. At the end of the performance, the lead actress, Raya Nagibzaba, talked to a reporter. "I wanted to show to the public that, at last, we have peace in Afghanistan. I hope that when people see this performance on television, they'll decide to visit the theatre." She was thinking about the massive Afghan refugee diaspora, some five-million strong. "I hope that fear will be expelled from their hearts, and that they will choose to serve their country."[3] Her speech, and other similar pronouncements, seemed persuasive: over two million refugees returned to Afghanistan in 2002.

Under UN auspices, ISAF (the International Security and Assistance Force) began its patrols in the capital in January 2002. "Everyone's very friendly" reported one Spanish officer, whose seventy-eight soldiers were greeted with shouts of 'welcome to Kabul!' from the local people as they toured the city.[4]

The international community quickly rallied round. At Tokyo in January 2002, sixty countries and eighteen international organisations promised help with reconstruction, pledging the colossal sum of $3bn in aid. Hamid Karzai, an elegantly-dressed Pushtun tribal leader, fluent in five languages, and with experience working for the American UNOCAL oil company, emerged as the temporary leader of a provisional administration. "We are committed to establishing a small, effective, disciplined security apparatus," he proclaimed, "that is accountable to the citizens and committed to respect universal human rights".[5] He kept his word, calling the Loya Jirga, a traditional tribal assembly, something like the Estates-General of Old Regime France, to ratify his administration and his leadership. 'Democracy born again in Kabul' smiled the *Guardian* headline, 'a Triumph for Karzai' proclaimed the *Figaro*.[6]

On 25th January 2002 Russian engineers re-opened the important Salang tunnel, blocked during fighting in 1998. This 2.7 kilometre-long tunnel runs north of Kabul and forms the principal route to connect the capital to the northern plains. It was originally built by the Soviets in 1960-64: cars and lorries queued impatiently on the day it was re-opened.[7] Markets and stalls opened across the country as the economy revived.

Other signs of a return to normality quickly emerged. In place of the Talibans' ban on all dancing and almost all music, Afghanis now listened to radios, cassettes and concerts. In Kabul, the older tradition of rich, glamourous wedding parties, with their long, loud sessions of music and dancing, was revived.[8] Britain's Football Association sent out trainers to assist the Afghan team prepare for the 2006 World Cup.[9]

48

Donald Rumsfeld spoke of Afghans "learning to play baseball instead of cowering in fear and hiding from the Taliban's religious beliefs".[10] Women were finally allowed to drive alone: the first new women drivers qualified in January 2003.[11]

Bernard-Henri Lévy, a French right-wing liberal, acted as the intellectual cheer-leader for the US-UK intervention. On 21st December 2001 he proclaimed "the liberation of Afghanistan" after the USA's one hundred day armada. The campaign had demonstrated that dictatorships were fragile, and the collapse of the Taliban marked "fundamentalism's first real defeat". "Fundamentalist zeal can do nothing against a B-52." The campaign was certainly not against Islam: indeed, it was another example of the USA helping Muslims.[12] Later, Margaret Thatcher joined him, noting the triumph of the USA's military assault on 'Islamic extremism', and welcoming the extension of this campaign to Iran, Syria, Iraq and North Korea. "The west as a whole needs to strengthen its resolve against rogue regimes and upgrade its defences. The good news is that America has a president who can offer the leadership necessary to do so."[13]

All these points suggest good news for the people of Afghanistan, who have suffered almost continual warfare since the Soviet invasion in 1979. Anyone would prefer peace, Bollywood and baseball to Communist or Taliban repression. Unfortunately, the optimistic reports of 2002 were misleading. Whatever the US-UK campaign has done, it has not liberated Afghanistan.

Looking back over the reports of the campaign, one notes some peculiar features. Unlike previous wars, it was difficult to follow the progress of this offensive on a map. While there were a number of set-piece battles around major cities, such as Kabul, Kandahar and Mazar-i-Sharif, elsewhere it was hard to be sure which were the 'liberated' areas and which were those still controlled by the Taliban. While there were many stunning shots of breathtakingly beautiful Afghan landscapes, there was little hard information about who was fighting who. The colossal devastating power of America's aircraft was repeatedly demonstrated, but at times it seemed almost as if their bombs and missiles were exploding in thin air. Certainly, the American commanders never spoke of military or civilian casualties.

Why did the Taliban collapse so easily? In October 2001, they had warned that they were prepared for a long war: their strategy was to leave the towns, and hide in the mountains.[14] Have they really just disappeared? If this was a war to liberate Afghanistan, then what was one to make of the leaflets dropped by US planes: 'Attention. You are condemned. Did you know that? The instant the terrorists you support took over our planes, you sentenced yourself to death.'[15] This sounded more like the language of Rambo than of George Washington.

Some of the results of this 'liberation' also look strange. If women are now 'allowed' to take off their *burqas*, then why do most women in Kabul still wear them outdoors? Unveiled or partly veiled women report being jostled, hit and spat on as they walk through public spaces. If this is a regime based on toleration and free speech, why is it that music stores and stalls are being threatened and even attacked? If reconstruction is proceeding apace, then why is that a Canadian Human Rights delegation, visiting Kabul in September 2002, reports that there is not a workyard or crane in sight?[16] If the Taliban and Al-Qaeda have been eliminated, then who is regularly firing rockets and grenades at US and ISAF forces in Afghanistan? One report estimates that there were twenty-two attacks from 18th to 28th January 2003, killing eleven US soldiers and injuring twenty-nine others.[17] Why are girls' schools suffering rocket attacks? Who are the local warlords to the south, the west and the north who take customs revenue, impose regulations and even issue their own currencies?

The media myth of the 'liberation of Afghanistan' was based on two fundamentally false propositions: a massive over-estimation of the

Taliban's strength *prior* to October 2001, and an equally exaggerated appreciation of Karzai's new powers *after* December 2001. To understand the shifting nature of political power in Afghanistan we need to take a step backwards, and consider the history and nature of this strange land.

BUILDING AFGHANISTAN

The first claim to rule the present-day territory of Afghanistan was issued by King Ahmad Shah in 1747. The task which lay before him was immense.

For centuries, this geographic zone has been a conduit for ideas, peoples and goods. Buddhism travelled from northern India to Asia through Afghanistan. The giant statues of standing Buddhas at Bamiyan were a testament to Buddhism's influence: they were blown up by the Taliban in August 2001. Alexander the Great and Genghis Khan both led invading forces into Afghan territory. Islam arrived from the west between the seventh and tenth centuries. Most Afghans followed the Sunni branch of this religion, and were then isolated from the Sunni centres in Saudi Arabia by the rise of Shi'ite Islam in Iran. In the thirteenth century, Marco Polo visited. His journey out of Europe followed the silk route established by merchants and traders to the far east. Polo noted the startling differences between the territory's deserts, its orchards, its fertile valleys and its bustling towns.

The new king's territory was a varied patchwork of ethnic groups, cultures and religious forms. The land itself seems equally irregular, formed into deep valleys, high mountains and broader plains out to the west. Indeed, Afghanistan's basic geographic pattern can be understood as one vast mountain range, the Hindu Kush, running down from the north-east to the south-west, with two broad valleys on either side. Aerial photos of the Afghan mountain ranges show a peculiar pattern: the land almost looks corrugated. Each fold can hide a new, fertile valley, and each valley can in turn host a different culture or ethnic group. One anthropologist estimated that there were fifty-five separate ethnic groups in Afghanistan, and another researcher found that thirty languages are spoken: it has inevitably been pointed out that even these exhaustive estimates simplify the situation.[18] This geographic structure often encouraged a type of territorially-based pluralism: there was always another valley available for a new group of migrants or invaders, creating more autonomies.[19] The final result is a web-like structure, capable of great resilience.[20]

Imposing any type of coherent political structure over this territory was going to be difficult. There is even some evidence that the largest cities and most extensive irrigation schemes in Afghan history can be dated to the period before the Mongol invasions of the thirteenth and fourteenth centuries, and that since then the area has grown more fragmented. In the nineteenth century, the Afghans were successful in repelling invaders, beating off the Russians and British (twice, in 1842 and 1880), and so creating a type of negative unity among the different populations against outsiders. Afghans are rightly proud of their ability to resist colonialisation. In 1919 their country was one of only three Muslim lands which were not controlled by Europeans (the other two being North Yemen and the area which was to become Saudi Arabia).[21] Developing a more positive sense of national unity, however, proved difficult. The territory itself had been formed by a working arrangement between the three nearest powers, it was "an empty space on the map that was not Persian, not Russian, not British".[22] While Islam is the religion of the vast majority of the Afghan population (there is also a small Sikh minority, a legacy of British colonialism), it did not in itself create a homogeneous national culture, for the native Afghan religious forms are highly localised, based around the tribal customs, village mullahs and local shrines.

King Abdur Rahman (1880-1901) attempted to impose a different model of political unification. Rahman conceded direction of Afghan foreign affairs to the British, in return for a subsidy and a promise of non-interference in Afghan internal affairs. In 1893, a British civil servant, Durand, traced out the border between Afghanistan and its southerly neighbours, now known as the Durand Line. Rahman attempted to exploit Islam by claiming a divine right to rule. Significantly, he used most of the British subsidy to build up the army, and in turn it was military organisations that pioneered the first modern industries in Afghanistan.[23] The civil service was rationalised, and for the first time some form of administrative unity was imposed on Afghanistan. The lasting legacy, however, of Rahman's rule was an awkward imbalance between outside sponsors and Afghan elites. Frequently, Afghan rulers and elites admired aspects of Western society, and wished to emulate them, but their interpretation of modernity was highly selective. Modernisation was not imposed from without by colonialist powers, but neither was it constructed from within: rather it spread almost haphazardly over Afghan society, following the traces and lines of central authority, sticking – above all – to military authorities. The resulting socio-economic pattern was unusual. Most colonial societies contain dual economies: one sector, usually more advanced, is orientated towards the colonial power's needs, while a second sector, generally quite primitive, serves the local populations. In Afghanistan, a different pattern emerged: the advanced sector was tiny, too small to encourage the growth of a local bourgeoisie, and it was quite unconnected with the wider Afghan society; it represented a type of de-terrritorialised economic modernity, arbitrarily scattered across the territory.

These juddering moves in turn created sporadic anti-central revolts but, more importantly, bred a widespread and permanent suspicion of the central state.

This uneasy relationship between Afghanistan and the outside world continued in the twentieth century. The Russian Revolution brought a new wave of migrants to northern Afghanistan, but by May 1921 the feudal Afghan monarchy had signed a Treaty of Friendship with the new Bolshevik state. Indeed, during the twentieth century, Afghanistan seemed to be courted by almost all the great powers, gaining a radio tower, mills, power plants and carpet factories from Nazi Germany, a massive, expensive and almost completely useless dam from the USA, and a deep road tunnel from the USSR.[24]

Afghanistan's varied ethnic and cultural groups can be classified, simply, as southerners and northerners. The south has historically been inhabited by Pushtuns, a tribal people, speaking their own language, Pushtu, whose affairs are regulated by their own unwritten customary code, the Pushtunwali. They are not confined to Afghanistan: Durand's 1893 line cut through their lands, and today many Afghan Pashtuns retain close links with Pakistani relatives. This explains, in part, the initial warm welcome given to Afghan refugees in Pakistan after 1979.[25] It also clarifies the ambiguous status of Peshawar, the first significant town over the Pakistan border on the road from Kabul. Peshawar exists in a type of legal-administrative no-man's-land between Afghanistan and Pakistan. It now functions as a centre for the reception of Afghan refugees, the headquarters for some of the world's most fearsome smuggling syndicates, and a base for the training of fundamentalist militia. Some evidence also indicates that an Al-Qaeda centre was established there in 1980.[26]

Over the past three centuries, the Pushtuns have been the rising force in Afghan society. They were principally farmers and herders, and in the south their social arrangements, while formally excluding women, were relatively egalitarian and even democratic, based on strong ideals of hospitality, consensus and cooperation. They normally live in small villages based around extended families.[27] However, the development of larger land-holdings, particularly in the centre and north, put a strain on these older ideals. A separate Pushtu land-owning class was formed.

As the Pushtuns expanded their influence over the central mountain range, they imposed more inegalitarian economic forms on tenants and labourers.

North of the central range are a more varied range of groups, tribes, and cultures. In the north-east corner are the Tajiks, whose lives are not organised along tribal lines. They speak Dari, a variant of the Persian language. The Uzbeks live to the north: they are farmers and herders. In the centre of Afghanistan are the Hazara, a more Chinese-looking people, who speak another variant of Persian, and who are Shi'ite Muslims. Aside from this important religious distinction, the Hazara seem noticeably different from other groups for a number of reasons: for generations they have been the victims of prejudices which often resemble racism. On occasion, this has led them to take a far more openly collective oppositional stance than other Afghan groups: a few of them were even successfully recruited by Maoists. More recently, the Hazara are the only group to have organised female soldiers and to have have provided some encouragement to politically active women.[28] One final peculiarity marks the Hazara out from other Afghan groups: they are the only people who live entirely contained within the country's borders; all the other ethnic and cultural groups spread over into neighbouring lands.

While each category can be defined according to religion, language and customs, there is another important geo-political dimension to these conflicting identities. Each looks to outside sponsors and patrons: the Pushtuns, firstly to Pakistan but – more recently – to the USA; the Uzbeks and Tajiks to the north, to the new republics of Central Asia and the Russian Federation; the Hazaras to China and to Iran, their co-religionists. Often these lines of patronage cut across ethnic, cultural and religious ties: this last point is vital, for it shows that – as yet – ethnicity has not become the principal force in the formation of political groups within Afghanistan.[29] When talking to Afghans about their country's tribes and cultures, I have found that they normally begin by identifying the main groups, then they list factors such as physical appearance, religion, language, tribal customs ... Then, frequently, they stop and sigh, commenting that a decade ago all this old nonsense seemed unimportant. The point here is that we must draw back from thinking of ethnic tensions as 'traditional': they are clearly new factors, created – or transformed – by the latest political stresses that Afghanistan has suffered. Arjun Appadurai's comments of outbreaks of ethnic violence in the 1990s are relevant here. He writes of globalisation creating "a world in which large-scale identities forcibly enter the local imagination and become dominant voice-overs in the traffic of ordinary life", and observes that ethnic conflict is best understood as an *implosion* of the outside world into daily life.[30] Something similar was happening in Afghanistan.

No accurate census exists of the relative size of these ethnic groups nor, indeed, of the total size of Afghanistan's population. This leads to some wild varieties in estimates, neatly pinpointed by Bernt Glatzer. While all observers concede that the Pushtuns are the biggest single group, notes Glatzer, the estimates of their proportion within Afghanistan range from as low as 40% to as high as 60%. Given that estimates of the total population range from fifteen to twenty million, this means that the total number of Afghan Pushtuns could be as low as six million or as high as twelve million.[31]

One last point needs to be made about Afghanistan's ethnic composition: Kabul is *different*. Situated just to the south of the main mountain range, this city of approximately six hundred thousand people in 1979 has acted as a meeting point for all cultures, ethnicities, tribes and religions. It was never a city dominated by a single language or culture. During the 1970s a new generation was growing up in Kabul: knowledgeable about the west, politically educated, often fluent in both Dari and Pushtu, considering cultural or ethic classifications as irrelevant and delighting in the city's cosmopolitan mixture. One nostalgic musician has described how he used to be able to walk through the musicians' quarter of the old city and, at each house he passed, he could hear types of music from each of the different Afghan regions and from further afield.

Kabul was also the site of Afghanistan's main university, which was the home for a range of Communist, secular, and Islamist groups. Predictably, it often acted as the vanguard of modernity for the rest of the country. This role stimulated some particular innovations: for example, prior to 1989, the *burqa*, the all-enveloping head-cover which the Taliban made compulsory for women, was very rarely worn on the streets of Kabul. The few women who did wear it were either rural women visiting the city or – according to legend – prostitutes who wished to hide their identities. A journey from the village to the city was also a journey through cultures and epochs: to conservative male village leaders, Kabul represented a threat to women, and therefore they encouraged women to wear the *burqa* to protect them from the city's influence. For the Taliban, capturing Kabul representing seizing control – and so stopping – the process of cultural, political and economic modernisation in Afghanistan. For this reason, they acted with particular ferocity in their policing of the city.

A NATION OF REFUGEES

Between five and six million people fled from Afghanistan during the 1980s.[32] In addition, there were about one and a half million Afghans who left their homes and sought refuge within Afghanistan. In other words, somewhere between one third and one half of the Afghan population were displaced in the 1980s; arguably, this was the largest flight of refugees ever in human history. Some returned in the 1990s, but frequently they would find that they were unable to stay, and meanwhile waves of new migrants joined the refugee camps. Even those who stayed in their homes in Afghanistan felt a clear sense of displacement and estrangement from the Communist, *mujahdin* and Taliban authorities: it could reasonably be argued that they felt *as if* they were refugees in their own homes.

The largest number – probably about three million – settled in Pakistan; the second most significant community, maybe about two million strong, stayed in Iran.[33] Aside from these groups, a significant number of middle-class professionals and intellectuals sought refuge in the West, and a few went to the Soviet Union, forming a global diaspora of displaced Afghan liberals. Their experiences as exiles often prolonged the paradoxical lessons they had previously learnt in foreign universities. As Sayd Bahaouddin Majrook notes, 'Marxist-trained intellectuals came mainly from the West and the anti-Marxists from the East'.[34] Of more long-term importance, however, was the experience of the bulk of the refugees, the peasants and traders who stayed in Pakistan and Iran. In dreadful circumstances, they were given some harsh lessons in the nature of contemporary globalisation, for to be a refugee today is to leave behind, if only temporarily, many of the comforting illusions provided by the structures of the nation-state and to enter the new zone of extraterritoriality.[35]

The Soviet occupation (1979-89) marked a radical departure from previous patterns of authority and development. While there were two rival pro-Soviet Communist Parties in Afghanistan, neither commanded the loyalty of the majority of the population. The reasons for the Soviet invasion of December 1979 are still disputed: did the Soviets fear the Chinese subversion of their Afghan satellite?[36] Or did the CIA supply Afghan tribes with weapons in 1979 in order to provoke the USSR into initiating a campaign which could not be won?[37] Or was control over the future distribution of oil supplies the motivating factor? Soviet policies, based on an atheist political culture and giving priority to developing an industrial base, were implemented ruthlessly in

Afghanistan. Opposition was simply not tolerated: traditions of provincial and local autonomy were ignored.

The Soviets gained some support in the main towns and in Kabul. They certainly engaged in extensive building works, constructing the houses in the elite Wazir Akbar Khan suburb which today serve to host officials from the UN, NGOs and national governments. They also built the massive Silo bakery in Kabul, which at its height employed two thousand workers and could produce 120,000 nan breads per day.[38] In particular, their governments were appreciated by some urban women, as Soviet rule opened up job opportunities and educational facilities to women: a point which has since persuaded some feminists to consider the Soviet occupation almost as a Golden Age in contemporary Afghan history.[39] Behind these real improvements in some women's lives, however, it should never be forgotten that this was a government based on an occupying army, serving foreign geo-political interests. While it suited the occupiers to recruit a more educated female workforce, they expanded facilities for women: if the regime's economic priorities had changed, its commitment to any sort of gender reform would also have been dropped. Secondly, alongside the tangible benefits experienced by urban women, it should not be forgotten that many rural women suffered disruption and economic decline as the Soviet regime attempted to enforce economic modernisation in the countryside.

The harsh nature of Soviet rule met with almost immediate resentment from most of Afghan society. Many considered that they faced a difficult choice: resist or flee. Of the eight hundred lecturers working at Kabul University in 1978, seventy-five were arrested and executed. Approximately five hundred and fifty left for the West. Twenty-five stayed in Peshawar, and about half of this small group joined the Afghan resistance to the Soviet occupation.[40] When an anti-Soviet rebellion erupted in Herat, in western Afghanistan, the Russians responded with a sustained bombing campaign which may have killed twenty thousand people.[41] Repression of this nature reveals the true nature of the Soviet occupation: it was not a liberation, but an attempt to exploit Afghanistan's geographic position for political ends.

Millions of Afghans suffered the degrading experience of becoming a refugee. As a generalisation, Afghans are a proud, self-reliant, independent people. One of the first reactions by refugee families when they acquired a tent, a self-built hut or some other temporary protection, was to put up some kind of fence or screen around their dwelling, to mark it out from the outside world and therefore assert their autonomy.[42] But being a refugee meant accepting a position of dependency on alien authorities, whose attitudes were often bewildering and sometimes hostile. It meant the loss of land, and therefore a rapid fall into poverty. In the search for alternative incomes, many turned to smuggling, which then drew drugs into the refugee communities.

Refugees in Pakistan sought to re-make the Pushtu culture with which most of them identified. In the absence of land and any viable income, this attempt to synthesise a cultural identity under adverse circumstances was invested with great significance. The role of women was particularly stressed: they had always been seen as representing the essence of Afghan culture, preserving its values and providing its symbols of honour. In this difficult environment, conservative tribal norms became reified, and male Afghans attempted to re-assert their authority by re-defining the camps: they saw "all spaces beyond the immediate vicinities of their homes as hostile worlds where women without male relatives [became] intolerably vulnerable".[43] Contacts with international relief agencies, offering limited health care and educational facilities, were fraught with tension and difficulty.

Women's responses to these strains are difficult to analyse, for the obvious reason that there was no public forum in which they could express themselves. For many, there can be no doubt that the simple, practical task of holding together their families occupied all their time.

Some may have considered the new Pushtun cultural conservatism unfortunate but appropriate. An articulate minority certainly protested and – according to some accounts – from their number RAWA (the Revolutionary Association of Women of Afghanistan) was formed.[44]

The origins of the Taliban, however, lie elsewhere. As the refugees spent ever longer in their camps "a generation of illiterate and uneducated youth" grew up.[45] These were young men who had never seen their 'native' villages, but who knew of them through the customary codes such as the Pushtunwali. Some commentators hoped that the common nature of this dreadful experience, in which Pushtun and Uzbek, Tajik and Hazara, all suffered, might be cathartic, and lead to a new sense of common Afghan nationalism.[46] There were attempts to form political parties among the exile communities, often inspired by the tolerant Sufi ideals which are common in Afghanistan. Given the fragmented nature of Afghan cultures, however, the formation of a united political voice was an intensely difficult task. At this point, outsiders made a decisive intervention. ISI (the Pakistani Intelligence services) wanted a stronger hold over the refugee groups. The CIA was interested in aiding the anti-Soviet resistance. In 1980 the Pakistan government demanded that the refugee parties merge to form no more than seven groups, who would act as conduits for aid.[47] The ISI and CIA then chose to support fundamentalist groups among the refugees.[48] This heavy external intervention permanently warped the nature of political culture among the refugees: their organisations were no longer orientated towards representing Afghans' grievances and aspirations, but to attracting foreign aid. They then won support from Afghans not by their policies, but by their ability to provide money and arms.[49] In other words, the spread and development of these apparently political organisations actually de-politicised the Afghan refugees.[50] Jonathan Neale, an experienced leftist commentator on Afghan politics noted in 1988 that "there was no party or group in Afghanistan that any decent person could support".[51] Initially, one might suspect he was being arrogant: in reality, Neale's comments accurately sum up the condition of Afghan political culture at the end of the 1980s.

Away from the seven political-religious parties, Saudi Arabian backers sponsored the development of *madrassas*, Islamic boys' schools, in which refugee children and orphans memorised the Koran through the repeated chanting of its verses. There, they heard "fanatical, superstitious speeches, full of the certainty drawn from ignorance".[52] These young men were separated from their mothers and sisters by increasingly strict regulations governing contacts between the sexes. Often their fathers were not in any position to guide them: they were dead, absent, or crushed by the strangeness of the long refugee experience. In other words, these primitive schools were often the strongest influences in these boys' lives.

In the 1980s, however, it was the seven religious-political parties which led the successful *mujahdin* offensive against the Soviet occupation. By 1985 they were armed with Stinger missiles, which proved highly effective against Soviet helicopters. The USSR army withdrew in 1989, but continued to supply a puppet government based in Kabul. In 1990 the CIA attempted to buy back its Stinger missiles: significantly, their offer was refused, and – to the intense annoyance of the State Department – some were eventually re-sold to Iran.[53]

Kabul was finally taken by the *mujahdin* in April 1992. This should have been a new beginning for all Afghanis. Refugees began to return from the camps in Iran and Pakistan. However, in place of a new nation, they found themselves caught up in a horrific bloodbath. The residents of Kabul tried to stay indoors as rival factions fought on the streets of their city. The weakness of the seven parties became quickly obvious: there was no common political platform, no links uniting the Sunni majority with the Shi'a minority, no nationally-agreed leadership, and the rival international patrons pursued different agenda.[54] No political principles were agreed on: military leaders "fought, switched sides and fought again in a bewildering array of alliances, betrayals and bloodshed".[55]

In place of Soviet centralised authoritarianism, Afghanistan was ruled by a new caste of warlords, each controlling his patch by terror and intimidation. These were rulers with no sense of direction, of ethics, of development strategies, but with a finely honed and well-tested ability to grasp which way the wind was blowing, plus an expert training in the art of modern warfare, using a bewildering mixture of medieval organisation and up-to-date technology, supplied with the blessings of the ISI and CIA. Increasingly, after their victories of 1989-92, their victims were civilians. According to Mary Kaldor, this type of warfare is not a peculiar Afghan aberration, but is actually typical of this new century. "Mobilising people is the aim of the war effort", she comments, "the point of the violence is not so much directed against the enemy; rather the aim is to expand networks of extremism".[56] Warfare was part of the ordinary exercise of power for these new elites. Their corruption was obvious: they organised the smuggling of drugs, arms and precious gems; they used protection rackets to steal property from ordinary Afghans; they fought among themselves in endless border disputes according to the rules of what Kaldor terms 'jihad culture'. Inherent in their rule was sexual abuse: according to one folk legend – which might be true – one of the first actions by the Taliban was to protect a young boy from rape by two *mujahdin* commanders who were fighting over him.

THE TALIBAN

The Taliban were born in this sorry, miserable, violent context. Afghans had been betrayed by foreign powers and by the new generation of *mujahdin* leaders. Approximately a million and a half people died between in violent conflicts in the 1980s and 90s.[57] But, also, the foreign powers were frustrated. Money and arms had flowed into Afghanistan.

Backer	Funds
USSR	$45 billion
USA	$4.5 billion
Saudi Arabia	$4.5 billion

Estimates of funds supplied to Afghan groups, 1980-92.[58]

Despite these massive efforts, there was still no stable government in Afghanistan: no possibility of building oil or gas pipelines, of stopping the flow of heroin out of the country, or of exploiting the region's resources. The continuing presence of the millions of Afghan refugees was a burden on the UN, Iran and Pakistan. ISI-CIA's decision to back the seven largely fundamentalist parties was clearly an error.

According to legend, in the spring of 1994 an obscure, one-eyed cleric, Mullah Mohammed Omar, led a group of about thirty young men, of whom only sixteen were armed with rifles, in an attack on the base of a warlord near Kandahar, in south-western Afghanistan.[59] His group was successful, and this first action was followed by further offensives. The Pakistani authorities rapidly grew interested. The trade routes north of Pakistan, into Iran or towards the Russian federation, had been effectively blocked by the warlords' banditry. Could this new group guarantee the security of roads? Even the Kabul government briefly considered that Omar's group could be a useful counter to the warlords' influence.

It is now well-known that Omar recruited from the Pakistani *madrassas*: his soldiers were virgins with Kalashnikovs, with no knowledge of maths, science, history or geography, no experience in trade or farming, no friendships with sisters, female relatives or any other women, but an intense, literal, simplistic acquaintance with the Koran. One can even debate whether they were 'fundamentalists': while the precise meaning of the term has been debated, experts tend to argue that it implies some commitment to both a purification of Islam of local traditions and to a universalistic ethic. These warriors were intensely localistic, loyal to an 'imagined tradition' drawn from the Pushtu villages from which they were exiled.[60] Often they were orphans: even when this was not the case, they usually came from shattered and depressed refugee families. To many Afghans they appeared as true innocents, radically different from the venal warlords. Their promise was not to seize power, but to end corruption.

This simple picture, however, is not entirely accurate. Among the Taliban ranks were some more politically experienced men: military advisors supplied by ISI (although the Pakistan government has been quick to deny this), and officers recruited from the old Soviet forces. While the warlords' previous campaigns had involved some acts of spectacular violence, their combats often seemed genuinely medieval: big on show, chants, and loud proclamations of bravery, weaker on sustained, co-ordinated military actions, and often marked by informal truces. The Taliban learnt modern military methods: they acquired tanks, and ISI helped them repair some ex-Soviet Mig fighters. Pakistani advisors trained them in night-time attacks. By January 1995 the Taliban commanded fifteen thousand trained soldiers, by December 1995, twenty-five thousand.[61]

More importantly still, when confronted with a genuinely powerful foe, such as the organised drug-smugglers of Helmand province, the Taliban became experts in exploiting the ancient Afghan military tradition of playing off rivals against each other. Afghans themselves joke about their contradictory attitudes to war and honour: as their saying goes, 'An Afghan can never be bought ... but he can be rented!' The Taliban turned bribery into 'a fine art'.[62] This point means that we should look carefully at the stories of the Taliban's easy victories. Certainly, by February 1995 they were beginning their long siege of Kabul, and by March 1995, after fighting for less than a year, they controlled twelve of Afghanistan's thirty-one provinces.[63] Kabul was finally taken by the Taliban, after bitter fighting and much new shelling of the devastated city, in September 1996. The open, public power of the marauding warlords was restrained, though never entirely smashed. The Taliban, however, never achieved complete control of Afghanistan. Even in the summer of 2001, Tajik and Uzbek soldiers of the Northern Alliance, formed from the remnants of the seven political-religious parties recognised by Pakistani government, were holding out in the north-east. There was also some resistance to Taliban rule by the Hazara in their central provinces. The Taliban felt a specific hatred for the Hazara, partly a radicalisation of the older Pushtun assertion of their political power, but partly also because the Hazara were Shi'ites. According to one report, some fifteen thousand Hazara were killed in a last-ditch gesture of Taliban authority in October and November 2001.[64]

The Taliban's main aim within Afghanistan was to break the secular cosmopolitanism which they saw as principally represented by Kabul. They therefore implemented a reign of terror over the city. Kabul football stadium was converted into an open-air execution arena: the heads, hands, and feet of the punished were publicly displayed there. Football matches were grudgingly allowed, but spectators were forbidden to cheer. Executions would be staged at half-time: no one was allowed to leave the stadium; applause was compulsory at this point. Musicians had to bury their instruments in order to preserve them; poets had to memorise their verses rather than write them; bookshop-owners, librarians, museum curators and archivists had to disguise their holdings. Boys' education was severely curtailed; girls' schools disappeared all together, sometimes replaced by illegal networks of home tutors. Above all, the Taliban were terrified that their soldiers might be seduced – literally and metaphorically – by the city's women, hence their ferocious restrictions on women's clothes, movements, work and even their visual presence: one Taliban decree insisted that if women were present in a room which could be seen from the street outside, then the room's windows were to be painted black.[65]

Paradoxically, these restrictions were often ignored in the villages. One can argue this point through on religious grounds: even in Kabul, the Taliban's guiding principle was to prevent contact between women and non-related men. In the small villages, everyone was some sort of relative to everyone else: therefore, no need to wear a *burqa*. More practically, the Afghan economy depends on women's agricultural work, most of which cannot be performed indoors. Insisting that all rural women permanently wear a small tent would have ruined the Afghan economy. (This point concerning the relative freedom of the villages was often missed by visiting western journalists during 2001-02, who tended to assume that if conditions were bad in Kabul, then they must be dreadful in the countryside.)

Acceptance of the Taliban's rule was often far more provisional and limited than the gory images from Kabul might suggest. In many rural areas of Afghanistan, life continued as before. In May 2002, US Special Forces interrogated fifty-five men from Hajibirgit, a small village in the west. They were asked about their attitudes to the previous regime: one of them replied that he could not say, as "the Taliban never came to our village".[66] Obviously, this may merely have been a convenient answer to give US interrogators, but it could have been the simple truth. It can be questioned whether, in reality, the Taliban ever formed an Afghan government. They remained scared of the capital city: Mullah Omar only visited Kabul once. Otherwise, he remained in Kandahar, which sometimes seemed to be functioning as a new capital. Lines of communication were confused, and orders from one department would often by counter-manded by another. The Taliban were sceptical about nationalism, considering it to be a foreign, secular concept. Significantly, on taking power in Kabul, they changed the name of 'Radio Afghanistan' to 'Radio Shari'a'. While never simply an ethnic grouping, the bulk of their leaders came from the Pushtun tribes, and it seems likely that ethnic prejudices exacerbated the violence shown in their offensives in the north of the country. How could a particularistic group like this ever command the loyalty of all the diverse Afghan cultures?

Aside from the obvious limitations of their political culture, the Taliban did not possess the administrative capacity needed to run a modern government. This point was very clearly brought home to me when I interviewed Ali Wardak in early in 2002. I asked why the Taliban, after ruling Kabul for over five years, had failed to begin any substantial reconstruction programme. Ali just laughed. "Can you imagine a *mullah* as Minister of Reconstruction? Can you imagine a *mullah* as Minister of Planning? He'd need some training in civil engineering, in planning. Administration? They know nothing about such matters."[67] A second illustration of the same point can be gained by examining the meeting of executives from Bridas, an Argentine-based oil and gas firm, with a Taliban delegation in February 1997 to discuss the possibility of constructing an oil pipeline in Taliban-controlled Afghanistan. Who did the Taliban choose to represent their interests? Twelve *mullahs*, of whom one had a qualification in engineering – but no practical experience in the field. Predictably, the negotiations did not reach a satisfactory conclusion.[68] Many Taliban warriors were illiterate: they could stride through the streets of Kabul, a Kalashnikov over one shoulder, an iron-cable whip in their other hand, lashing out at passers-by who they considered broke the Taliban's rigid dress codes, but they were unable to check identity papers.

Many of the ordinary functions of government – roads, public works, economic co-ordination and planning, construction – simply ceased while the Taliban were in power. Other areas – education, health care – were in effect contracted out to NGOs.

Yet this oppressive, incompetent and intolerant clique came to power because of Pakistani backing and American complacency. For a long period, successive US administrations remained terrifyingly naïve about the Taliban. Some US diplomats saw them as an Oriental equivalent to born-again Christians![69] The majority view throughout the 1990s was to tolerate any regime which would allow the UNOCAL oil company to pursue its plans to develop pipelines crossing Afghan territory; or to treat Afghanistan as 'Pipelineistan'.[70]

All this began to change in 1996. The UN and the EU both expressed concern about the repression that women suffered under the Taliban. In 1997 Madeleine Albright visited a refugee camp in Pakistan, and knelt down to talk to a group of Afghan children. "I'll never forget you – being with you," she told them, "I will do everything to help you to help your country".[71] In 1998, American feminists led a protest campaign about UNOCAL's activities in Afghanistan. The Clinton administration, reliant on women's votes, showed some sympathy. RAWA played a small but important role in this development: it was often the conduit through which American feminists learnt of Afghanistan. The dialogue between American feminists and politically active Afghan women, however, was not always successful. Outside observers seized on the *burqa* as the central issue, the key to women's oppression. Afghanis often replied that this was not the issue which concerned them most.[72]

A POST-MODERN WAR

Who knows the reasons for the Bush administration's decision to begin military operations in Afghanistan in October 2001? None of the hijackers involved in the 11th September attack came from Afghanistan. Was Afghanistan attacked because Osama Bin Laden had set up training camps in the country? Because the Taliban refused to co-operate with the US attempts to extradite him? Because of the frustration felt by companies such as UNOCAL with the Taliban's inability to co-operate? Or was it simply the need to be *seen* to be 'fighting terrorism'? After all, which other country was going to defend the Taliban regime?

The initial plan was simple: a massive bombing campaign would terrorise the Afghans into submission. The offensive was planned to avoid two unacceptable options: as far as possible, there were to be no American casualties, and the US administration was not to get involved in the tiresome process of 'nation-building'. With a little initial reluctance, the American military authorities accepted the need to use Northern Alliance soldiers as their infantry, but retained misgivings about allowing them to capture Kabul. The final aim was to produce a more reliable partner to replace the troublesome Taliban regime.

This campaign marked the beginning of the 'war against terrorism': it therefore effectively defined what this 'war' meant to the Bush administration. It was understood, crudely, as a *military* campaign. There was almost no attempt to persuade Afghans, Arabs, Asians or Muslims of the justice of the USA's actions: no cultural or political dimension to the campaign was considered. Secondly, there were no discussions of the causes of Bin Laden's popularity, or of socio-economic action which might win over the masses of Arabs or Asians to respect the USA as a force for beneficial development. Richard Sennett, the respected American sociologist, wrote a short article within days of the 11th September attack. Much of it was undistinguished, but it included one short comment that probably sums up an important dilemma far better than many longer pieces. "I have no idea how to fight terrorists effectively. I suspect our rulers do not, either."[73] In other words, it may well be a mistake to study the US campaign as an expression of some carefully considered masterplan. The Bush administration were acting on instinct, reducing some of the most complex dilemmas faced by polities in the contemporary world to a simple security problem to be resolved by vigorous police action.

These factors gave the Afghan campaign its radically new features, so different from the accepted norms of modern warfare. This was not a conflict in which one nation faced another. On the one hand, it can be disputed whether the Taliban genuinely constituted a 'national' government or represented a nation and – secondly – the Americans' war was supposedly with Al-Qaeda, not the government of Afghanistan. But, on the other hand, even the Americans adopted new techniques: in place of the citizen-soldiery, that backbone of republican nations from Sparta to Private Ryan, the USA fought the war by proxies – B-52's and Northern Alliance soldiers. It was hard to see what principles, if any, were at stake: what did the 'liberation' of Afghanistan mean in practice? Simply the violent removal of the Taliban?

After the first three weeks of the bombing campaign, even the Americans were baffled. On 25th October 2001, Condoleeza Rice, Bush's National Security Advisor, noted: "We've bombed everything we can think of to bomb ... and still nothing is happening."[74] The Taliban seemed more confident than ever. Would the US have to resort to sending in thousands of American troops? The final weapon, which ultimately won the campaign, was the use of bribery: $50,000 was usually enough to persuade a local military leader to defect, and the adroit expenditure of $70m ultimately won the war. Bush was impressed: "That's one bargain," he commented. But bribery brought nothing new to Afghanistan: as has been shown, the Taliban made use of precisely the same tactic in their advances. Its advantage is that it avoids loss of life. Its disadvantage is that it can never create a political or ethical legitimacy for a new regime. Within RAWA's vituperative polemics, there was one short, six-word phrase which pin-pointed the true nature of the conflict between the USA and the Taliban: "a fracas between patron and ex-protégés."[75] In other words, the only principles at stake here were those of power and authority: would the USA be able to enforce its rule?

Just as the Taliban seemed to melt away before the American onslaught, so the new administration would appear equally insubstantial when faced with the dilemmas of running a country. The campaign's peculiar features added to the decades of de-moralisation and de-politicisation suffered by Afghans.

This was a war of B-52s against Kalashnikovs: it was no surprise that the Taliban retreated. While almost anyone would welcome the end of the Taliban regime, the military campaign could not, by any stretch of the imagination, be termed a *liberation* of the country. To cite RAWA once more: "one fundamentalist band cannot be fought by siding with and supporting another."[76] In other words, the simple destruction of the Taliban's political power cannot, in itself, be equated with the liberation of Afghanistan as there has been no substantial change in the deeper power structure.

The Taliban, however, were never defeated. They left the towns: zones which they had never truly controlled. Many fled southwards, over the border to Pakistan. Others moved into the central mountains, and waited. As far as possible, they avoided direct confrontation with the international forces, but they re-emerged late in 2002, particularly in the south-east of Afghanistan, firing rockets and grenades at US posts.

In the absence of a truly decisive military engagement, in the absence of a genuine political mobilisation of the majority of the Afghan population, it was difficult to demonstrate the reality of a victory. This was no accident. The US leaders, always aware of the dangers of negative reporting, carefully steered reporters away from truly important topics which could illustrate the real nature of this campaign. Incidents and issues such as the massacre of Taliban by the US ally Dostum in Mazar-i-Sharif, the number of unexploded bombs left in fields by their aircraft, the killing of civilians, the intelligence bungles, the use of torture on prisoners and the possible use of non-depleted Uranium-tipped weapons were all kept away from the public's gaze.[77] The confusing encounters at Tora Bora in December 2001, Chah-i-Kot in March 2002 (known as Operation Anaconda) and at Spin Boldak in January 2003 did not provide clear, *visual*, proof of the US-UK's victory: in these cases, the enemy (Taliban? Al-Qaeda?) managed to slip away, leaving behind them a few corpses and a little rubbish.

For these reasons, there was a sustained search for symbols which could be used to illustrate the progress of the campaign. The smallest sign or gesture began to take on an awesome symbolic weight. Women without *burqas*, men without beards, wedding parties, Bollywood videos and – according to Donald Rumsfeld – baseball were all applauded by a western press desperate for some decisive evidence of the victory. Polly Toynbee even argued that women wearing high heels are "like the first defiant glimmer of victory".[78] Such trivialising attitudes can arouse fury among the Afghans. "You can't feed yourself by shaving, can you?", retorted one man.[79] RAWA scorned those Afghans who played along, mocking the rapid make-over that the Northern Alliance leaders had undergone. "Their ridiculous newly-acquired obsession with their 'civilised' appearance and their aping of the latest European menswear" could not erase their bloody military record.[80] Rather than demonstrating the 'liberation' of Afghanistan, these points suggest quite the opposite: there had been no substantial change in the real nature of political power.

The previous structure of modern military conflicts, as definitively analysed by Clausewitz, threw one nation-state against another, entailing a mobilisation of resources, people and economies. They began with a formal declaration of war and ended with a peace treaty. In Afghanistan, the conflict was post-modern in nature: not the trendy post-modernity celebrated by some cultural critics' erudite phrases, but a more gritty, gory, mud-spattered, destitute condition. Significantly, the US-UK offensive could not even be satisfactorily named: was it a Crusade? A war? A liberation? An occupation? The combatants did not fight for principles, they played an intricate game with power structures. It was not about things, but about appearances. There were no truths to reveal, merely layer upon layer of deceptive interpretations. To the victor went the prize: the ability to manipulate images, successfully … for a while.

At least three thousand civilians, probably more, were killed by the US-UK offensive.[81] Some fifteen hundred cluster bombs were dropped:

from these, there remained an estimated fourteen thousand unexploded bomblets on the ground in March 2002.[82] Millions took the roads, fleeing from the renewed fighting. Some returned, once more, to the camps in Pakistan and Iran. The country was suffering from a severe drought, its people already weak from malnutrition, and so prone to disease.

The Taliban vanished, and the Northern Alliance commanders moved in to Kabul. The city's people braced themselves for a repetition of the bloody conflicts of 1992-96: there were ugly stories of armed robberies, car-jackings and mafia-style murders in the 'liberated' city.[83] The main problem was that many of the Alliance soldiers had not been paid for months, and they considered that having won the war, they were entitled to the prizes which the city offered. By the end of January 2002, however, the Northern Alliance withdrew its men from the city.

KARZAI'S GAMBLE – NATIONHOOD AND RECONSTRUCTION

Hamid Karzai returned to Afghanistan on 13th December 2001. In many important ways, the problems he faced were similar to those faced by King Ahmad Shah in 1747: a divided country, with little to unite it in any positive sense. The key differences were that in 2001, external forces were operating with far greater violence, and an existing socio-economic infrastructure has been devastated by two and a half decades of war. According to one estimate, only about 12% of people living in cities have access to safe water. Natural resources have also been ruined: in 1977 55% of Badghis province, in the north-west, was forested, as was 37% of Takhar province, in the north-east. In 2002, satellite cameras could find hardly any evidence of trees in either province.[84]

Karzai has always presented a clear programme: his aim is the reconstruction of the country through co-operation with the international community and through the long-term implementation of democratic structures. To this end, he wanted a stable Afghan currency (finally created on 2nd January 2003) and a national army.[85] His public pronouncements are confident and statesmanlike, frequently stressing the moral unity of an Afghanistan re-born after the decades of civil war. "There will be no ethnic war in Afghanistan", he stated in March 2002, "Afghans are more united than you think. Afghanistan's national identity and its dignity have been restored."[86] "The refugees are coming back. It is a proud moment for me … We need security, we need peace, we need stability, we need an administration in control of all Afghanistan."[87] "We are a nation, a united nation. There are individual [opponents] perhaps, but believe me, as a nation we are one."[88] One might consider that his aims are modest, even banal: nothing more than an Afghan imitation of the dominant models of the constitutional nation state. In the words of the UN representative, Lakhdar Brahimi, Karzai's new administration aimed simply "to reconstruct national unity, to re-make the state, and to extend the state's authority".[89] The problem is that even such an apparently banal ambition is almost impossible to achieve in today's Afghanistan.

When we turn to examine power politics, the difficulties which Karzai faces become clearer. His first priority was security. Some progress has been made in disarming the nation. One estimate calculates that ISAF personnel have 'removed and neutralised' 175,000 military items since December 2001.[90] But these steps do not, in themselves, allow Karzai to constitute a new nation-state: to survive, his government needs its own armed forces. Until this is done, Karzai has consistently called for the extension of ISAF beyond Kabul as an interim measure.[91] This proposal has always been refused by the allies, although in January 2003 the USA did begin to send out army patrols on humanitarian missions, such as re-building bridges, into the Afghan provinces.[92]

Karzai's eloquent, confident statements disguised a more worrying situation. The country he sought to re-build was in ruins. The buildings which were to house the new ministers in Kabul had "no heating, no electricity, no chairs, no offices, no telephones. Some even had no doors or windows."[93] Yet these officials were supposed to re-create the nation's central administration from this rubble! Beginning this process was an immensely difficult task: difficult, firstly, because of this simple lack of the most basic resources but, more importantly, difficult also because each resource problem had a political dimension. RAWA correctly commented: "In a country like Afghanistan where there is no trace of a legal infrastructure or even a quasi-democratic government, most social and economic issues must be addressed as political issues."[94]

Some indication of the economic context within which these new officials worked can be gained by considering relative rates of pay.

- $1 per day: typical wage for a member of a mine-clearing team
- $2.20 per month: standard pension for a disabled Afghan war veteran (usually unpaid)
- $15-30 per day: typical wages paid to a heroin smuggler
- $40 per month: average salary of an official in a government ministry, November 2002
- $50 per month: salary for a soldier in the new Afghan army
- $75 per year: average income of a Kabul resident
- $200 per day: pay for Afghan mercenaries fighting for US forces at Chah-i-Kot, March 2002
- $2,000 - $3,000 per month: typical rents paid by UN and NGO officials for a house in Kabul
- $6,500: income earned from 14 kg of raw opium extracted from poppies from one farm

The Economy of the New Afghanistan[95]

The lesson from these figures is very simple. Afghans who want to make money will find it easier to get rich by growing opium poppies, providing services for the new UN-NGO elite residing in Kabul or by serving as mercenaries for US-directed military initiatives than they will by clearing mines, working in a ministry or trying to get a job in Kabul. While the Afghan economy has revived slightly since October 2001, this is largely because it simply could not have been more depressed. As yet, the mass of Afghan people have experienced very little benefit from the promised aid from the international community and, in particular regions, returning refugees are suffering worse than ever.

Definitive figures for the amount of aid that Afghanistan has received are hard to find.

Source	Money pledged	Money delivered
Guardian, October 2002	$4bn	$0.4bn
Reuters, October 2002	$5.25bn	$1.4bn
New York Times, December 2002		$1.8bn

Estimates of aid to post-Taliban Afghanistan[96]

One point is clear: according to almost every estimate, the amount of money delivered has been significantly less than the amount promised. There was a telling incident in 2002. RAWA appealed for outside funds to create an Afghan women's university to train teachers and medical personnel. The response was so disappointing that plans to build a college had to be shelved, and instead RAWA turned to considering developing long-distance learning facilities.[97] Afghans regularly complain that now the Taliban regime has gone, they have been forgotten by the rich nations of the world.

Still, one billion dollars or so sounds like a lot of money. What has happened to it? Many of these global estimates fail to distinguish between the money sent to the new Afghan government, and that donated to UN agencies or NGOs active in Afghanistan. (There are now over one thousand such agencies in Kabul alone.) According to another estimate, over half the aid received has gone to the latter.[98] While these agencies are usually motivated by a real concern for the country's plight, their practices have often had the unintended effect of perpetuating relationships of dependency. For example, until September 2002, not one of them employed an Afghan woman in an official capacity. Another telling example is the supply of computers, which are nearly always set up for use in English – so that reports can be written for the agencies' headquarters – but not in Dari or Pushtu.[99] These agencies have also found it hard to operate under Afghan conditions, and often make their first priority the purchase of suitable transport vehicles. The result? New traffic jams and air pollution in Kabul. When questioned on this point, the Afghan Minister of Public Works erupted in fury. "Stand outside my window and you'll see two hundred white Land Cruisers pass by in an hour, I swear it!"[100]

More seriously, Afghanistan's first, desperate, need is simply for food for the estimated seven million people who are threatened by famine and drought.[101] (According to one estimate, the water flow in Afghanistan's biggest river, the Helmand, has shrunk to 2% of normal in recent years.)[102] Aid money is swallowed up by these emergencies, and is rarely used for more long-term development or reconstruction programmes. The return of refugees has often made matters worse. They flocked to Kabul, excited by the promise of reconstruction offered by the Loya Jirga. From a city of some six hundred thousand in 1979, over three million people live there now.[103] Their presence is pushing up rents and exhausting scarce food supplies.

The simple weakness of the Karzai government has been repeatedly demonstrated. The thirty-one countries associated with the Bonn Accords of December 2001 have noted this. They complained a year later than Karzai has not made enough progress in re-making his country.[104] In February 2003, one expert considered that "it will be in the best interests of refugees to remain where they are" rather than attempt to return to Afghanistan.[105] There have also been some more spectacular examples of the limits to Karzai's powers. Two ministers have been murdered (in February 2002 and July 2002) and Karzai himself was the victim of an assassination attempt (in September 2002). No one has been arrested for these crimes, and rumours circulate that these attacks were actually ordered by rival ministers. The sight of Karzai protected by bodyguards supplied by the USA is an eloquent indication of his real position. Karzai has been quite open about his regime's vulnerability, stating in one interview: "If America left next month, Afghanistan would be in a shambles."[106] The best that can be said about this terrifying situation is that Karzai is forced to act by conciliation and persuasion. While he remains little more than a symbol of power, it is less likely that he will be attacked, or, in the words of the *Financial Times*, "Karzai is surviving because he is so weak".[107]

Paradoxically, one consequence of this weakness can sometimes be a tough, repressive policy. On 11th November 2002, a group of about two hundred and fifty students from Kabul university organised a demonstration about electricity cuts and the cancellation of meals in their dormitories. They intended to march on the Presidential Palace in Kabul. The police stopped them. When the students refused to disperse, the police fired at them, killing three and wounding more than twenty. Students returned to protest the next morning, and were again met by police violence. Some of the wounded were taken to hospital: police then toured the wards, warning the students not to speak to the press.[108]

The reason for this violent, heavy-handed approach appears to be a government fear that the students' protest could be exploited by the Taliban opposition. The action, however, demonstrates the fragility of the Karzai regime, in which even hungry students are treated as seriously as if they were armed terrorists.

The murders, assassination attempts and police brutality point to the shallowness of Karzai's hold on power in the capital. Outside Kabul, his government often appears non-existent. One can measure his weakness simply by counting soldiers. By December 2002, the new Afghan National Army had only 1,360 recruits: many had already deserted. According to one estimate, there are between seventy-five thousand and one hundred thousand soldiers in the warlords' militias, plus approximately another hundred thousand armed men with military experience who are not currently enrolled in any militia.[109] This disparity in forces has been made yet worse by the US policy of employing mercenaries, who were usually supplied by warlords, and generally better paid than the soldiers in the 'national' army. Following the brief battle at Spin Boldak, on the Pakistan-Afghanistan border, in January 2003, one Afghan government official was able to inspect the base of an anti-government rebel. He was amazed. "We are the government and we don't have any food, but he has many, many sheep, telephones and a wireless! Three motorbikes! He had a better life than us!"[110] The final indignity is the role of Mohammed Fahim, the Minister of Defence. Fahim maintains his own private army and stockpile of weapons in the Panjshir valley, in the north-east. His Jamiat-e Islam faction has recently negotiated a $40m military helicopter deal with Russia.[111] At the same time, Fahim works to prevent the formation of the Afghan national army.[112]

Out in the west, in the town of Herat, is the warlord Ismail Khan's fiefdom. He commands approximately twenty-five thousand soldiers.[113] Khan's power exemplifies all that has gone wrong in Afghanistan. He is a highly experienced Tajik commander: although a Sunni Muslim, he has been generously supplied with weapons by Shi'ite Iran. He fought the Soviets in the 1980s, and the Taliban in the 1990s, and took refuge in Iran when defeated. During the 1990s he occasionally appeared more liberal than the Taliban, and on occasion would boast of his promotion of women's schooling. But since 2001 his rule, based on 'a virtual mini-state', has become increasingly repressive.[114] Pushtuns are a particular target for police repression; women are forced to wear the *burqa*; men are not allowed to wear ties; the press is subject to increasingly rigid censorship; music cassettes and videos are publicly burnt; reports of the routine use of torture in Herat's prisons circulate. There is also a reported spate of self-immolation among girls in Herat: perhaps three cases per week, over a hundred in 2002. Impoverished families are arranging marriages. Often their daughters are told to become the second or third wife of a rich man. In Herat, however, the girls are often from families who took refuge in Iran, where they became influenced by that country's notoriously liberal sexual attitudes. The girls protest against their impossible situation with these acts of spectacularly defiant self-destruction.[115]

Yet, astonishingly, Donald Rumsfeld made an official visit to Herat on 29th April 2002, and later commented that Khan was "an appealing person ... thoughtful, measured and self-confident." As ruler of the district, Khan takes $1m per day in customs duties on trade between Afghanistan and Iran.[116]

Regrettably, Khan is not a tragic exception. In the south, Kandahar is ruled by the warlord Haji Gul Agha Shirzai and the cleric Naguibullah, to the north Abdul Rachid Dostum and Ustad Atta Mohammad battle for control of the region around Mazar-i-Sharif, while Jalabad in the east is run by Haji Abdul Qadir. Each runs their particular region more or less as a separate state. Looking closely, one can distinguish some differences in their rule: in Kandahar, the dominant impression is of a return to the 'normality' of the Taliban, while in the north, anti-Pushtun measures are implemented.[117] In November 2002, twenty-two private papers were edited from Mazar-i-Sharif in the north, two or three struggled to survive in Herat, while none at all were permitted in fundamentalist Kandahar.[118] The overall impression, however, is that much of Afghanistan is ruled by a new caste of intolerant, repressive warlords.

It is said that every flea carries with it a host of little fleas. So it is with Afghan warlords: around each regional warlord is a host of local commanders. For example, Fatoullah Khan commands the area around Kaysar, in the north-west. He is one of Dostum's men, and can rehearse some horrific stories concerning the cruelty of the Taliban. For how long has he fought for Dostum? "Forever. He is a great man. Whatever he thinks, we think. Whatever he says, we say."[119] These words are worth some consideration. Fatoullah Khan is not a stupid man: he started his career as a soldier at the age of fifteen, in 1980. He has successively fought Russians, Pushtuns and Taliban. He has now risen to a position where he commands a thousand men, including three hundred cavalry. He also controls the economy of the area through a well-practiced protection racket, which concentrates on extracting money and food from the Pustuns living in his zone. His men follow the UN grain distribution, threatening the villages after each visit, stealing the grain. In another life, Fatoullah Khan could have been a significant middle level bureaucrat, perhaps the head of a regional development agency. But in Afghanistan he is simply a great thief. Even after his hard-won experience in military tactics, banditry and extortion, his political education is non-existent. Despite his eloquence, he is unable to utter the slightest political criticism of the Taliban: he merely criticises their cruelty in order to justify Dostum and his cruelty.

This system of major regional warlords and minor commanders is insidious and well-rooted: it is capable of frustrating the best efforts of NGOs and UN agencies; it is even capable of surviving the most fearsome attacks by the armed might of the USA.

Afghans have quickly realised how limited is Karzai's power. 'Karzai is the mayor of Kabul', runs one joke, while another states that 'Karzai is not President: the B-52 is President'.[120] President Musharref of Pakistan is publicly dismissive of Karzai's hopes to make Afghanistan into a modern nation-state: he considers that the country "is a tribal land, a tribal environment, in which the warlords control different zones."[121]

Karzai's rudimentary police forces are unable to guarantee security. Attacks on UN vehicles are increasing in the north, the centre and the south-west: in the first eight months of 2002 there were at least seventy serious incidents of this type.[122] Banditry is growing more common. In February 2003, the UN High Commissioner for Refugees announced a suspension of the projects in the area south of Kabul, as a result of the repeated attacks on UN personnel.[123]

Karzai's orders are frequently ignored. In November 2002 he attempted a show of force: he dismissed twenty generals, intelligence officials and local commanders from their posts.[124] Many of them simply refused to leave. As for the growth of liberal democratic values? There are many signs that authoritarian and repressive politics are returning. Even within Karzai's administration, these tendencies can be observed: the Chief Justice, Maulavi Fazel Hadi Shinwari has recently declared that co-education is "in contradiction to Islamic law", and has issued orders to close down Kabul's five cable television stations.[125] The case of Sima Samar, the female chair of the new government's Human Rights Commission, provides another telling illustration of the nature of political power in the new Afghanistan. In June 2002 she was arrested and accused of blasphemy, as a result of some reported remarks by her which may have questioned the nature of *shari'a* law. This accusation is extremely serious: it could result in capital punishment. The court showed every sign that it would reach a guilty verdict, until Karzai's personal intervention: it then reached the decision that it did not have sufficient proofs to reach a conclusion.[126]

Elsewhere there are increasing signs of a revival of sympathy for the Taliban and their repressive politics, particularly in the areas south of Kabul and in the south-west, around Kandahar. Musicians are beaten up in Shakardara, ten miles from Kabul, by men implementing a

Taliban-style ban on music.[127] Girls' schools are subject to rocket attacks in Wardak province, just west of Kabul.[128] Gulbuddin Hekmetyar, another warlord with decades of experience, preaches *jihad* against the Karzai government and the US occupation. His Arabic-language pamphlets have been circulating in south-east Afghanistan since September 2002.[129]

This desperate situation explains Karzai's turn to the Loya Jirga. In the absence of any other power base, this traditional institution was used to provide the new government with some form of legitimacy. Its convocation was also a practical demonstration of the Karzai's own political strategy: he wished to show Afghans that he was familiar with the country's political traditions and that he would respect them. It was a means for him to reach out to ordinary Afghans.[130] The Loya Jirga met in June 2002, and voted overwhelmingly to confirm Karzai as head of state. The position of the ministers belonging to the Northern Alliance, however, was not challenged. Outside observers noted that in many areas voters were intimidated and some candidates prevented from participating.[131]

The new government does not appear to have acquired legitimacy. It has therefore been unable to come to terms with the country's past, nor to plan properly for its future. No programme of investigation of past crimes has been planned: there is no Afghan equivalent to the invaluable South African 'Truth and Reconciliation' committee. Past warlords, tyrants and butchers still operate with impunity.[132] It is left to UN investigators to consider Afghanistan's bloody past. The patient, tireless activity of the heroic Pakistani lawyer, Asma Jahangir, has been particularly commendable in this field.[133] Attempts to plan for the future have also foundered. The Human Rights Commission has no nationwide presence, the Civil Service Commission is not functioning and the Judicial Commission was disbanded in February 2002, to be re-constituted in November 2002. One key debate concerns the future constitution. In December 2001 there was a loose consensus around the idea that Afghanistan should return to the largely liberal-secular constitution of 1964. During the course of 2002, this proposal was challenged with increasing strength by a vociferous Islamic lobby, which demanded that *shari'a* should recognised as the basis of Afghan law. It is hard to see how these two viewpoints can be accommodated in the same constitution.

Karzai's project is to re-constitute Afghanistan as a modern nation-state. The few resources that he holds are those of the nation-state: his power is strongest in the capital, his government is the recipient of international aid, and – potentially – it should be able to offer Afghans work, education and a focus for their hopes. At present, his main enemies are the warlords, operating with their ruthless, stripped-down approach to political power and patronage, and their post-modern attitude to political ethics. The combat between the two closely resembles other conflicts in the world, between older forms of community and new, globalised, forces of destruction.

RE-VEILING AFGHANISTAN

Afghans have grown tired of the presence of foreigners in their country. While they realise that aid is absolutely essential to help them survive the continuing drought, they curse, indiscriminately, both the 'Arabs' who arrived with the Taliban and who dragged them into this latest international cycle of blood-letting and revenge, and the 'Americans' whose planes dropped another crop of bombs of their fields, whose helicopters circle, engaged in an ever-more desperate search for phantom terrorists, and whose soldiers patrol their streets. A certain xenophobia is developing among many Afghans, perhaps merely the unpleasant underside of a more positive sense of Afghan national identity.

And yet ... more foreigners visit: drought investigators, drugs police, environmental researchers, Human Rights officials, restaurant managers (one does operate in Kabul for the UN-NGO elite), educational co-ordinators and surveyors plus a fresh crop of anthropologists, archaeologists, sociologists and musicologists. And all of them want to talk about 'the veil'. Sometimes it seems as if every second newspaper article, academic essay and book is entitled 'unveiling Afghanistan', 'behind the veil', and so on. What 'veil'? The leather-and-brass beaked masks of rich Saudi women? The thin cotton gauze which seems to float over the heads of Egyptian air hostesses? The tcha-Dior, paraded by the fashionable bourgeoises of Tehran? No: the *burqa*, the now near-universally recognised symbol of some absolute oppression of women.

Against the *burqa*, another universal constant: the mini-skirt. "Kabul's golden age was in the 1970s," writes one journalist, "Those were the days when many women wore miniskirts."[134]

This is commentary reduced to the most rudimentary form of stigmatisation. To reply properly would require a volume: let us merely rehearse a few simple arguments. The peoples around the eastern and southern shores of the Mediterranean and in west Asia have worn various forms of head-coverings for millennia. The traditional depiction of Mary, the mother of Jesus, normally shows her with her head covered. Veils, in different forms, have been most frequently by women, but there are interesting exceptions such as the veils worn by male Tuaregs.[135] The practice is not unchanging: veils and veiling develop according to shifts in politics, cultures and religious practices. They are therefore the most visible symbols of deeper processes.

Peter Marsden's comments on the Taliban's policies are relevant at this point:

Afghanistan is one of the few places left in the world where the Western media do not penetrate to a significant degree. The rigidity of the Taliban gender policies could be seen as a desperate attempt to keep out that other world, and to protect Afghan women from influences that could weaken the society from within.[136]

In other words, the *burqa* was not an arbitrary act of oppression, but part of an isolationist ethic. The ruthless violence with which the Taliban imposed their repressive dress code on the women of Kabul was clearly wrong. But it ought to be remembered that compulsory un-veiling may also be equally wrong. 'Compulsory', in this sense, could include a consistent, senseless and ignorant derision of the other by an institution with a degree of power – a state, an NGO, a UN agency – as well as legislative action.

Let's get our priorities right. First, food and shelter; next, education, jobs, prospects, debates; and then we can consider the veil. When they feel the time is right, Afghan women will act to change the way they dress.

Until then, an aphorism: To wear a *burqa* is not necessarily a sign of some absolute repression; to wear a mini-skirt is not necessarily a sign of some absolute liberty.

HEROIN – THE GOLDEN FLY

Half-way through Emile Zola's *Nana*, an epic saga concerning the rise and fall of a Parisian prostitute, there is a genuinely surprising passage: a story within a story, in which Zola appears to be summarising his own plot. The inner story, *The Golden Fly*, tells of a girl descended from four or five generations of drunkards, her blood tainted by drink and poverty, who grows up in the Parisian slums. Like a flower on a dungheap, she was tall and beautiful. "With her the rottenness that was allowed to ferment among the lower classes was rising to the surface and rotting the aristocracy." Acting instinctively, she was like a golden fly "buzzing, dancing and glittering like a precious stone, entering palaces through the windows and poisoning the men inside, simply by settling on them."[137]

The political implications of this parable take a while to unpick. Zola was no socialist: indeed, the whole of his work aimed to out-flank and contain the growing French socialist movement. In this passage, however, we seem to get something like a recognition of a class struggle, not waged by a politically conscious proletariat, but unfolding like a primitive, natural force. Zola is warning his middle-class readership of the inherent social dangers of a divided society: the new working-class cannot be simply 'contained' in their slums; their influence will spread out to infect the rest of French society.

Afghanistan has produced its own Golden Fly: since the fall of the Taliban, it has regained its position as the world's number one producer of heroin. In their last years, the Taliban, perhaps in one last desperate gesture to win a degree of international sympathy, implemented a sustained crackdown on heroin production. The amount harvested in 2000-01 was far lower than in previous years. In 2001-02, however, farmers turned back to opium cultivation. From 1994-2000, sales of opium brought in about $150m per year to Afghanistan: about $750 per family involved. In 2002, sales of opium brought in $1.2bn: $6,500 per family.[138]

There are many routes taken by smugglers out of Afghanistan, but the most common is eastwards, over the two thousand kilometre long border with Iran.[139] The Iranians have mobilised a force of some forty-two thousand soldiers, militiamen and police to patrol this border. A type of low-intensity war is fought out here: between 1979 and 2001 3,140 Iranians died along this frontier – about one every three days. In recent months, however, there are indications that the Iranians are losing this war. Following the arms embargo announced by Bush's famous 'Axis of Evil' speech, the Iranians are no longer able to supply their border guards with up-to-date military equipment. On the other hand, the Afghan smugglers have no difficulty in acquiring the most fearsome weapons. In 2002, the Iranians were probably only intercepting between a fifth and a tenth of the opium arriving on their eastern border.

The growth in the use of heroin across Central Asia leads to another serious problem. Addicts share unclean needles, and these bring about the extremely rapid growth of HIV/AIDS in the region.[140]

There is no obvious solution to this issue. While there is a ready and growing market for heroin in the West and Central Asia, while the new government is unable to enforce bans on the cultivation of opium poppies, and while poverty-stricken Afghan farmers are able to earn far more from opium cultivation than from growing food, the golden fly will flourish.

FOUR FUTURES FOR AFGHANISTAN

The battle for Afghanistan's future is clearly not a binary struggle between two equally opposed forces: instead, it involves different factors, interacting with each other. This situation makes it extremely difficult to predict the country's future.

In place of concluding with one forecast, I will present four.

TRANS-FEDERALISM

It will not be possible to create a nation-state in Afghanistan: in fact, while some previous Afghan regimes have managed to set up an approximate administrative unity, none has managed to create a nation-state, in the fullest sense of the term. In other words, there has never been that effectively unified national consciousness, that sense of identity between people and government that has sometimes marked the political culture of western nations over the past two centuries. The reasons for this are not difficult to find. Very few countries in the Middle East have developed into nation-states on the west European model: Iran and Turkey are perhaps the two closest equivalents. Instead, the Middle East is marked by trans-national cultures: Arabic is spoken from Morocco to Iraq; Islam is practiced from Morocco to Indonesia. The violent processes of colonialisation, national liberation struggles and de-colonialisation have created cultural and social tensions which make the creation of viable nation-states still more difficult.

It therefore seems unlikely that this new government will create a viable nation-state in Afghanistan. Instead, a more appropriate aim would be to federate the various forms of polities that exist in the country: the semi-autonomous tribal communities, the fledging regional and ethnic centres, the ethical and legal structures provided by local Muslim traditions, the mobilising capacities of the political groups, the public sphere, and the administrative capacities of the modern state. Such a project, as can be seen, is not a simple federation of different territories, but more a cultural federation of different civilisations.[141]

For such a federation to work, it would have to be based on persuasion and willing consent. For Karzai to succeed in this project, he would require the wisdom of a Tolstoy, the cunning of a Machiavelli, the charisma of *subcommandante* Marcos and the dogged determination of an Iranian feminist. It's a lot to ask of any individual … in fact, clearly too much. Such a project would require the willing, active participation of the bulk of the Afghan population; it could not rely on the expertise of a single individual. So far, Karzai has been singularly ineffective in encouraging such democratic mobilisations. His reliance on ISAF as a substitute army and his misplaced pride in the fledging Afghan army suggest authoritarian impulses.

Is it simply utopian to imagine such an outcome? Perhaps so: but there are two possible inspirations for this 'trans-federalism'. Firstly, the

Afghan people have been given a crushingly emphatic lesson in the vices of intolerance and factionalism. They feel an overwhelmingly deep desire for some better manner to organise their lives: perhaps from their pain will be born a new polity, less centralised, more humane than previous regimes. Secondly, throughout debates on Afghan political culture, women are the great unknown. Without access to the public sphere, their thoughts and wishes are easily ignored. Isolated reports reveal, however, some indications of vast female sub-cultures, organised around subterfuge and deception, away from the gaze of male authorities.[142] Most of them appear to be, understandably, pretty sceptical about established political projects. Karzai's rule has allowed some women to participate publicly in political debates: there were 160 women among the 1,551 delegates at the Loya Jirga. Still more promising, perhaps, was the launching in 2002 of *Effat* ('Courage'), a UNESCO-backed monthly which aimed to create an inter-regional dialogue among women.

Certainly, this option may appear utopian: but it is probably the only project which could guarantee Afghanistan's political stability in the future.

STATE-NATIONALISM

If Karzai fails to convince through persuasion, he may still succeed in defeating the opposition through the mobilisation of the resources of the nation-state. B-52s, ISAF and the new Afghan army may be able to win crushing military defeats over the warlords and therefore shatter their powers. Aid money could be used to finance the massive reconstruction projects that Afghanistan needs: militiamen could put down their Kalashnikovs and pick up pens.

The key difficulty here is that Karzai's autonomy would be severely compromised: reliant on the military might of the USA to win his military victories, he would be in a weak position to refuse any demands that were made of his regime. Afghanistan would become 'Pipelineistan'. Voices that were critical of the USA would be pushed out of the public sphere: American economic power rarely favours democratic, critical debate.

The indigenous anti-statism of the Afghans would still be a factor. Afghans would resent the re-structuring of their economy to suit foreign interests, and they would still consider the Afghan state as alien presence in their society. The various polities and proto-polities would not be working in harmony with each other and, once Karzai's charisma had faded, political stability would once again be threatened.

THE WARLORDS' RETURN

Karzai's power is limited: balanced between Pushtuns who resent the prominence of Tajiks and Uzbeks in the government, and Tajiks and Uzbeks who are united solely in their desire to prevent the return to power of a Pushtun oligarchy. The US government will realise that 'nation-building' in Afghanistan is too great a task even for the world's sole remaining superpower, and the B-52s will return to base. The one or two thousand men of the new Afghan army will not be sufficient to defend the regime.

The warlords' return will probably result in the effective dismemberment of Afghanistan, for there would no longer be any reason to have a national government. Eventually, the warlords' fiefdoms would be re-fashioned to square with ethnic identities, and they would proclaim loyalties to invented ethnic traditions as a de-politicised means to create a sense of unity. Maybe informal zones of influence, controlled by Pakistan, the Russian Federation and Iran, would be formed. Or maybe there would be a full territorial re-configuration of the nation. Kabul would become a divided city, like

92

Beirut in the 1980s or Jerusalem today, bitterly fought over as a symbol of a lost unity.

Politically, Afghanistan would become a wilderness: home-grown forms of authoritarianism, with loose references to the excesses of High Stalinism and to the misogyny and daily cruelties of fundamentalism, would thrive.

THE TALIBANS' RETURN

In the absence of clear governmental legitimacy, in the absence of reconciliation with the past and planning for the future, in the absence of any meaningful sense of political hope, the Taliban will return. They will be accepted as a symbol of Afghan independence from the outside world: their cultural and social repression will be welcomed as an alternative to chaos of the warlords' rule. They will have learnt nothing, forgiven nothing and forgotten nothing: their revived rule will be marked by vicious revenge attacks on all groups who were seen to oppose them. Refugees will flee out to Iran, perhaps to Russia and the north, and even out to the west. Perhaps the Taliban will initiate some form of administrative training, so that the framework of a functioning state might be created.

The lamp will then go out, and there will be only darkness in Afghanistan.

CONCLUSION

Liberating Afghanistan

If a super-sensitive spy satellite, directed by a stubbornly painstaking operator, had flown over Kabul one night in the 1970s it might have picked up the merest glimmer of a flickering light from the bedroom window of a silent house. Further investigation would have revealed a bizarre situation within the room: a young woman was reading at her table. The light came from a candle – but in order to hide her activities, she had draped a blanket over herself and the candle. She was in a dangerous position: her blanket could easily catch light. On the other hand, if her fundamentalist father caught her during one of his regular night-time patrols of the house, she risked an extremely violent beating. Yet, night after night, she continued reading grimy photocopies of Marx, Lenin, Machiavelli ... [143]

Why did she take such risks? She believed that she had devised a cultural strategy for her own liberation and for millions of women like her. Reading would lead her to knowledge, knowledge to empowerment, empowerment to liberation.

In 2001, the US-UK offensive proposed a different strategy for the liberation of Afghanistan. Hi-tech military hard-ware would devastate the Taliban centres; Northern Alliance soldiers and mercenaries would prevent their return. Within this schema, liberation was equated to the simple, physical destruction of an enemy's political and military power. 'Attention. You are condemned. Did you know that? The instant the terrorists you support took over our planes, you sentenced yourself to death.'

Instead of liberation, the offensive created an ethical, political and administrative vacuum which – as I write – remains unfilled. The most likely future for Afghanistan is a weak, rigid and intolerant nation-state acting as a façade for warlords and other fanatics. This will concern us: not so much by the creation of terrorist networks, but by the country's involvement in heroin production, international smuggling and AIDS-HIV epidemics, not to mention the continued cultural and social oppression and exploitation of a whole people.

These problems can only be solved by genuinely democratic forms, and democracy cannot be dropped from a B-52. In place of the post-modern, de-politicised cycle of power struggles which has battered Afghanistan for a quarter of a century, we must initiate a liberatory globalisation which will take the blanket from the candle. The shadows will still be there, but they will no longer be so frightening.

1. 'Abdul Malik', *Guardian*, 31st December 2001.

2. Many Afghan specialists argue that *chaderi* is the correct Afghan term. As readers are probably more familiar with the term *burqa,* I use it in this essay.

3. 'Teatro entre las ruines de Kabul', *El País*, 9th January 2002.

4. 'Los soldados españoles patrullan por primera vez las calles de Kabul', *El País*, 30th January 2002.

5. '$3bn in aid lays foundation for re-building', *Guardian*, 22nd January 2002.

6. 'Democracy born again in Kabul', *Guardian*, 14th June 2002; 'Le Triomphe de Karzai', *Figaro*, 20th June 2002.

7. 'Au nord de Kaboul: le tunnel de Salang', *Monde*, 25th January 2002.

8. 'Kabul succumbs to the wedding daze', *Washington Post*, 12th November 2002.

9. 'Blair backs Afghanistan's World Cup dream', *Guardian*, 8th August 2002.

10. Quoted on 'Building a Nation', *Newshour*, 20th August 2002.

11. 'Afghanistan: Women Drivers take to the Street', UN Office for the Coordination of Humanitarian Affairs, www.irinnews.org, 21st January 2003.

12. 'Ce que nous avons appris depuis le 11 septembre', *Monde*, 21st December 2001.

13. 'Islamism is the new bolshevism', *Guardian*, 12th February 2002

14. 'Los Talibán preparan a sus tropas para una "dura lucha" con Estados Unidos', *El País*, 1st October 2001; 'Notre terrain, c'est la montagne', *Libération*, 19th October 2001.

15. Quoted in 'The US Message to the Taliban', *Guardian*, 27th October 2001.

16. Ariane Brunet and Isabelle Solon Helal, 'Rapport de mission de Droits et Démocratie; septembre 2002', at afghana.org

17. 'Afghanistan Boils as Mujahideen carry out 22 attacks in last ten days', www2.jihadunspun.net, 29th January 2003.

18. Estimates in Bernt Glatzer, 'Is Afghanistan on the Brink of Ethnic and Tribal Disintegration?', in W. Maley (ed), *Fundamentalism Reborn?* (London: Hurst, 1998), pages 167-81 and Richard Newell, *The Politics of Afghanistan* (Ithaca: Cornell University Press, 1972), page 13.

19. Newell, *Afghanistan*, pages 24-25

20. See William Maley, 'Introduction: Interpreting the Taliban' in his *Fundamentalism Reborn?*, page 5.

21. Latif Lakdar, 'Why the Reversion to Islamic Archaism' in J. Rothschild (ed), *Khamsin: An Anthology* (London: Al Saqi, 1984), pages 275-301 (page 282).

22. Nick Cullather, 'Damming Afghanistan: Modernisation in a Buffer State', *Journal of American History* 89:2 (2002), pages 512-37 (page 515).

23. Newell, pages 44-47.

24. See the excellent article by Nick Cullather, 'Damming Afghanistan: Modernisation in a Buffer State'.

25. Inger W. Boeson, 'Honour in Exile: continuity and change among Afghan Refugees' in E. W. Anderson and N. H. Dupree (ed's), *The Cultural Basis of Afghan Nationalism* (London: Pinter, 1990), pages 160-74.

26. Olivier Roy, *L'Islam mondialisé* (Paris: Seuil, 2002), page 187

27. These comments on Afghanistan's ethnic profile are drawn from Ali Wardak, 'The Ethnic and Tribal Composition of Afghan Society', in E. Girardet (ed), *Afghanistan* (Geneva and Dublin: ICHR and Crosslines, 1998), pages 78-91, and Alfred Janata, 'Afghanistan: the ethnic dimension' in Anderson and Dupree (eds), *Cultural Basis,* pages 60-70.

28. Ahmed Rashid, *Taliban: the Story of the Afghan Warlords* (London: Pan, 2001), page 69

29. See Glatzer, 'Is Afghanistan on the brink ... ?'.

30. Arjun Appadurai, *Modernity at Large: Cultural Dimensions of Globalisation* (Minneapolis: University of Minnesota Press, 1996), pages 154-55.

31. Glatzer, 'Is Afghanistan on the brink ... ?', page 169.

32. According to Susanne Schmeidl, the number of refugees reached its peak of 6.2 million in 1989. See her '(Human) security dilemmas: long-term implications of the Afghan refugee crisis', *Third World Quarterly* 23:1 (2002), pages 7-29.

33. See Sabahudin Kushkaki, 'Afghan refugees: the Afghan View' in Anderson and Dupree (eds), *The Cultural Basis*, pages 115-20.

34. On the experiences of these groups, see the eloquent essay by Sayd Bahaouddin Majrook, 'Afghan Intellectuals in Exile: philosophical and psychological dimensions' in Anderson and Dupree, *Cultural Basis*, pages 71-83 (page 78).

35. See Zygmunt Bauman, 'Reconnaissance Wars on the Planetary Frontier', *Theory, Culture and Society,* 19:4 (2002), pages 81-90 (page 85).

36. Antonio Carlo, 'Afghanistan, Poland and Peaceful Co-existence', *Telos* 47 (1981), pages 56-65.

37. John Prados, 'Notes on the CIA's Secret War in Afghanistan', *Journal of American History* 89:2 (2002), pages 466-71.

38. 'People Plead for Water and Electricity', *Guardian*, 22nd January 2002.

39. See, for example, Christine Delphy, 'Une guerre pour les femmes?', *Monde Diplomatique*, March 2002; Valentine M. Moghadam, 'Patriarchy, the Taleban and the Politics of Public Space in Afghanistan', *Women's Studies International Forum* 25:1 (2002), pages 19-31; and Polly Toynbee, 'Was it worth it?', *Guardian*, 13th November 2002.

40. Majrooh, 'Afghan Intellectuals', page 80.

41. Rashid, *Taliban*, page 37.

42. Boesen, 'Honour in Exile', page 168.

43. Nancy Dupree, 'A socio-cultural dimension: Afghan women refugees in Pakistan', in Anderson and Dupree (eds), *Cultural Basis*, pages 121-33 (page 121).

44. Significantly, Dupree's 'Socio-cultural dimension', published in 1990, does briefly mention RAWA (page 129).

45. Kushkaki, 'Afghan refugees', page 118.

46. This suggestion forms the conclusion of Wardak, `Ethnic and Tribal Composition', page 91.

47. Peter Marsden, *The Taliban: War and Religion in Afghanistan* (London: Zed, 2002), page 28.

48. Rashid, *Taliban*, page 86.

49. Rashid, *Taliban*, page 19.

50. William Maley, 'Introduction' to his *Fundamentalism Reborn?*, pages 1-27 (page 9).

51. Cited in his later essay 'The Long Torment of Afghanistan', *International Socialism* 93 (2001), pages 31-59.

52. Tiziano Terzani, *Lettres contre la guerre* (Paris: Liana Levi, 2002), translated by F.G. Batlle, page 70.

53. John Prados, 'Notes of the CIA's Secret War in Afghanistan', *Journal of American History* 89:2 (2002), pages 466-71.

54. See Amin Saikal, 'The Rabbani Government, 1992-96' in Maley, *Fundamentalism Reborn?*, pages 29-42.

55. Rashid, *Taliban*, page 21.

56. On 'new wars', see her provocative and perceptive essay, 'Beyond Militarism, Arms Race and Arms Control', ssrc.org/sept11

57. Rashid, *Taliban*, page 18. The following paragraphs owe much to Rashid's authoritative work.

58. Rashid, *Taliban*, page 18.

59. See the account in Rashid, *Taliban*, pages 23-26.

60. For example, William Maley considers that they might better be termed 'traditionalist' than 'fundamentalist'. See his 'Interpreting the Taliban', pages 18-20. On

the other hand, Roy classifies that as 'neo-fundamentalist': see his *Islam mondialisé*, pages 133-84.

61. Anthony Davis, 'How the Taliban became a military force' in Maley (ed), *Fundamentalism Reborn?*, pages 43-71 (page 60).

62. Rashid, *Taliban*, page 35.

63. Rashid, *Taliban*, page 31.

64. 'Pits reveal evidence of massacre by Taliban', *Guardian*, 8th April 2002.

65. Nancy H. Dupree, 'Afghan Women under the Taliban' in Maley (ed), *Fundamentalism Reborn?*, pages 145-66.

66. 'One Year on in Afghanistan', *Independent*, 5th August 2002.

67. 'An Afghan Optimist' – interview of Ali Wardak, *Planet: the Welsh Internationalist* 151 (February 2002), pages 7-16 (page 12).

68. Rashid, *Taliban*, page 170.

69. Rashid, *Taliban*, page 177.

70. US policies are coherently analysed in Richard MacKenzie, 'The United States and the Taliban', in Maley (ed), *Fundamentalism Reborn?*, pages 90-103. The term 'Pipelineistan' is used in Howard J. Ehrlich, 'No Way to Peace: the First Six Months of the War against Terrorism' *Social Anarchism* 32 (2002), pages 22-41.

71. Cited in MacKenzie, 'The United States', page 90.

72. A telling illustration of this unsuccessful dialogue is provided by Sonali Kolhatkar, '"Saving" Afghan Women', www.zmag.org, 9th May 2002. See also Sedef Arat-Koc, 'Imperial Wars or Benevolent Interventions?– Reflections on "Global Feminism" Post September 11th', *Atlantis* 26:2 (2002), pages 53-65.

73. 'This time, one country indivisible', *Guardian*, 17th September 2001.

74. Cited in 'The $70m War', *Sunday Times*, 1st December 2002.

75. RAWA, 'Let us struggle against war and fundamentalism', www.zmag.org, 22nd March 2002.

76. RAWA, 'Let us struggle against war and fundamentalism'.

77. On torture, see 'CIA accused of torture at Bagram base', *Guardian*, 27th December 2002. On the use of non-depleted uranium, see 'UMRC's Project: Afghanistan – Field Investigation and Sample Collection Team's Report – Trip # 2', January 2003, www.umrc.net.

78. 'Was it worth it?', *Guardian*, 13th November 2002.

79. 'Al Qaeda not defeated one year on', Reuters, 10th November 2002.

80. RAWA, 'Let us struggle against war and fundamentalism'.

81. 'Storm over Afghan civilian victims', *Guardian*, 12th February 2002; 'Counting the Dead', *Guardian*, 8th August 2002.

82. 'Afghanistan littered with 14,000 unexploded bomblets, says UN', *Guardian*, 23rd March 2002.

83. 'Gun Terror of Kabul's liberators', *Observer*, 13th January 2002.

84. 'Afghanistan's Environment ravaged by war', Environmental News Service, ens-news.com/ens, 8th February 2003.

85. 'Hamid Karzaï: Equilibriste surdoué', *L'Express*, 17th January 2002.

86. Cited in 'Optimisme de l'Afghan Karzaï à Paris', *Libération*, 2nd March 2002.

87. 'Democracy born again in Kabul', *Guardian*, 14th June 2002.

88. 'Karzai defies vision of a divided country', Associated Press, 11th November 2002.

89. 'L'Afghanistan à l'heure de la reconstruction', *Libération*, 10th June 2002.

90. 'ISAF asks the world to abide by Afghan pledges', *Daily Times* (Pakistan), 9th February 2003.

91. 'Les Afghans veulent un renforcement de la force internationale', *Monde*, 1st February 2002.

92. 'Afganistán, primer año de paz', *El País*, 7th October 2002; 'Afghanistan: les réservistes américains s'engagent dans l'humanitaire', *Monde*, 16th January 2003.

93. 'Hamid Karzaï: Equilibriste surdoué', *L'Express*, 21st January 2002.

94. 'Let us struggle against war and fundamentalism'.

95. Sources: 'Un périple Afghan', aghana.org, 18th December 2002; 'Assaut américain contre un réduit taliban', *Libération*, 4th March 2002; 'Sur les routes de l'opium afghan', *Monde diplomatique* (March 2002), pages 6-7; 'Was it worth it?', *Guardian*, 13th November 2002; 'Le retour hésistant de la diaspora afghane', *Monde* 21st November 2002; 'Kabul adds Western style at a Price', Associated Press, 25th November 2002; 'Karzaï contra los "señores de la guerra"', *El País*, 15th August 2002; 'Old Fears in the new Afghanistan', *New York Times*, 8th December 2002; 'Afghanistan: Focus on Poppy Eradication', UN Office for the Coordination of Humanitarian Affairs, www.irinnews.org, 21st January 2003; 'Disabled Afghan War Vets Protest in Kabul', Associated Press, 14th January 2003.

96. 'Old Fears in the New Afghanistan', *New York Times*, 8th December 2002; 'Plea for Help', *Guardian*, 1st October 2002; 'Cash-strapped Afghans issue warning', Reuters, 24 October 2002.

97. 'Lack of donors scuppers Afghan women's project', *Times Higher Education Supplement*, 9th August 2002.

98. 'Afghans: world reneged on promises', Associated Press, 12th November 2002.

99. Brunet and Helal, 'Rapport de mission de Droits et démocratie'. The Canadian-based 'Droits et démocratie' was the first to employ a female Afghan as a representative.

100. 'Was it worth it?', *Guardian*, 13th November 2002.

101. 'Short backs military move to restore order in Afghanistan', *Guardian*, 11th December 2002; 'Our City, Our Future, in our Hands', *THES*, 24th January 2003.

102. 'Afghanistan's environment ravaged by war', Environmental New Service, ens-news.com/ens, 8th February 2003.

103. 'Le retour hésitant de la diaspora afghane', *Monde*, 21st November 2002.

104. 'Hamid Karzaï est invité à mettre de l'ordre en Afghanistan', *Monde*, 4th December 2002.

105. Cited in 'Afghanistan: Continuing Repatriation could cause destabilisation, says NGM', UN Office for the Coordination of Humanitarian Affairs, irinnews.org, 7th February 2003.

106. Cited in 'Building a Nation', *Newshour*, 20th August 2002.

107. 'Karzai's presence felt more strongly abroad than at home', *Financial Times*, 23rd December 2002.

108. 'Afghanistan: Police Beat Students in Hospital', Human Rights Watch, hrw.org/press/2002, 14th November 2002.

109. 'Toujours présent, le mollah Omar tente de fédérer les force d'opposition', *Monde*, 4th December 2002; 'Karzai, contra los "señores de la guerra"', *El País*, 15th August 2002.

110. 'Afghan rebels find recruits and sympathy in wild south', Reuters, 31st January 2003.

111. 'Afghanistan: Analysts say some neighbours interfering in Kabul's internal affairs', Radio Free Europe / Radio Liberty, www.rferl.org, 7th February 2003.

112. 'Karzai defies vision of a divided country', Associated Press, 11th November 2002.

113. 'Warlords are Afghanistan's New Worry Number One', Reuters, 12th December 2002.

114. The material in the succeeding paragraphs owes much to the invaluable report, 'All Our Hopes are Crushed: Violence and Repression in Western Afghanistan', Human Rights Watch, hrw.org/press/2002, October 2002

115. 'Self-Immolations on Rise in Afghanistan', *Los Angeles Times*, 18th November 2002.

116. 'Old Fears in New Afghanistan', *New York Times*, 8th December 2002. The figure of $1m is Karzai's own estimate.

117. '¿Dónde se esconden los talibanes?', *El País*, 12th August 2002.

118. 'Press Situation', Reporters sans frontières, rawa.fancymarketing.net/press, 13th November 2002.

119. 'Fatoullah Khan, roi des menteurs', *Le Figaro*, 31st July 2002.

120. 'Karzai struggles to establish control over Afghanistan', *Kansas City Star*, 21st January 2003.

121. 'Musharref débine le gouvernement afghan', *Libération*, 21st August 2002.

122. 'Afghan anarchy hinders aid', *Observer*, 1st September 2002.

123. 'Fresh attacks on UN in Afghanistan', ABC Online, abc.net.au, 2nd February 2003.

124. 'Karzai defies vision of a divided country', Associated Press, 11th November 2002.

125. 'Cable TV Un-Islamic, says Afghan judge', Reuters, 21st January 2003; 'Afghanistan: government to investigate female education in Herat', UN Office for the Coordination of Humanitarian Affairs, www.irinnews.org, 28th January 2003.

126. Brunet and Helal, 'Rapport de mission de Droits et démocratie'; 'Female Minister is "Afghan Rushdie"', *Guardian*, 18th June 2002.

127. 'Two dead, dozens hurt by grenades at Afghan wedding party', Reuters, 19th October 2002.

128. 'Afghan fundamentalists raid girls' schools', *Guardian*, 1st November 2002.

129. 'Karzai's Foes may be re-organizing', Associated Press, 6th September 2002.

130. On the symbolic importance of Jirgas in Afghan society, see Ali Wardak, 'Jirga: A Traditional Mechanism of Conflict Resolution in Afghanistan', http://www.institute-for-afghan-studies.org/ This text includes a detailed and critical preliminary assessment of the degree to which this latest Loya Jirga can be considered a success.

131. 'Afghanistan: the Return of the Warlords', Human Rights Watch, June 2002.

132. International Crisis Group, 'Afghanistan: Judicial Reform and Transitional Justice', www.intl-crisis-group.org, 28th January 2003. The points made in this section are largely drawn from this invaluable report.

133. See 'UN Investigator visits Afghan mass graves', Reuters, 20th October 2002.

134. 'Heard the one about the Afghan comedy show?', *Guardian*, 2nd January 2003.

135. On the veil, see Fadwa El Guindi, *Veil: Modesty, Privacy and Resistance* (Oxford: Berg, 1999). The male veil is discussed on pages 117-28. While I cannot accept all the arguments presented by El Guindi, her work is undoubtedly one of the most sustained considerations of the practice. An older, but still thought-provoking, essay is that by Franz Fanon, 'Unveiling Algeria' in his *Studies in a Dying Colonialism*, translated by H. Chevalier (London: Earthscan, 1989), pages 36-68.

136. Marsden, *Taliban*, page 99.

137. Emile Zola, *Nana* translated by G. Holden (Harmondsworth: Penguin, 1972), page 221.

138. 'Rising Drug Flow out of Afghanistan threatens Central Asian neighbours', Eurasianet.org, 6th February 2003.

139. Information in this section is taken from the highly informative article by Cédric Gouverneur, 'Sur les routes de l'opium afghan', *Monde Diplomatique*, March 2002, pages 6-7.

140. 'Rising Drug Flow out of Afghanistan threatens Central Asian Neighbors', www.eurasianet.org, 6th February 2003.

141. M. Nazif Shahrani has rehearsed similar arguments in a number of essays. In each case, however, his writing is marked by over-emphasis on the deficencies within Pushtu culture thus, for example, writing off the potential of their *jirga* tradition. See his 'The Future of the State and the Structure of Community Governance in Afghanistan' in Maley (ed), *Fundamentalism Reborn,* and 'War, Factionalism and the State in Afghanistan', *American Anthropologist* 104:3 (2002), pages 715-22. See, by contrast, the interesting considerations on Jirga's potential in Wardak, 'Jirga: A traditional mechanism'. On the political implications of tribal Islam, see Harold Barclay, 'Islam, Muslim societies and anarchy', *Anarchist Studies* 10:2 (2002), pages 105-18.

142. See, for example, Batya Swift Yasgur (ed), *Behind the Burqa: our life in Afghanistan* (Hoboken: John Wiley, 2002).

143. Yasgur, *Behind the Burqa,* pages 33-39.

Freedom Press also publishes the fortnightly
anarchist paper *Freedom*.
Contact us at the address below for the current
subscription rates and a copy of our booklist:
FREEDOM PRESS
84b Whitechapel High Street, London E1 7QX